Liberal Arts and Community

MARION MONTGOMERY

Liberal Arts and Community | The Feeding of the Larger Body

Louisiana State University Press   *Baton Rouge and London*

Copyright © 1990 by Louisiana State University Press
All rights reserved
Manufactured in the United States of America
First printing
99 98 97 96 95 94 93 92 91 90   5 4 3 2 1

Designer: Laura Roubique Gleason
Typeface: Primer
Typesetter: G & S Typesetters, Inc.
Printer and binder: Thomson-Shore, Inc.

Library of Congress Cataloging-in-Publication Data

Montgomery, Marion.
    Liberal arts and community : the feeding of the larger body /
    Marion Montgomery.
        p.   cm.
    ISBN 0-8071-1558-4 (alk. paper)
        1. Humanities.   2. Humanities—Social aspects.   I. Title.
AZ221.M66   1989
001.3—dc20   89-12792
                                                       CIP

To my teachers and students: past, present, and future

Polonius. What do you read, my lord?

Hamlet. Words, words, words.

Pol. What is the matter, my lord?

Ham. Between who?

Pol. I mean, the matter that you read, my lord.

Ham. Slanders, sir; for the satiric rogue says here that old men have grey beards.

Let the words of my mouth, and the meditation of my heart, be alway acceptable in thy sight, O Lord, my strength and my redeemer.

—Psalm 19

If I were to bring you food for your stomachs, you would divide it among you and no individual would get the entire amount. Furthermore, in proportion as you are more numerous, you would divide according as the number of those receiving would be increased. . . . Whatever I say is intended as a whole for all and for each individually. Behold how it is not possible to give a satisfactory explanation of the power which the human word possesses!

—St. Augustine

Contents

Preface   xi

I | Liberal Arts: The Sorting of Clichés   1

II | Nurturing the Mind: The Liberal Arts as Heart with Head   31

III | Liberal Arts and the Spiritual Confluence of Community   81

IV | The Quest for Community Ground: A Scholastic Foray   119

Index   165

Preface

The subject I would advance here invites platitude, as any good subject will. Platitude is less than exciting; but it is also likely to be more than dull when recovered to its origins. A truth abandoned because mouthed without conviction is no less a truth. But to attempt its recovery through spectacle of language—the metaphors and analogies and excessive reductions of complexities—is an additional temptation, a temptation with its own dangers. My cautionary note is that one must neither reject a truth because it seems worn out nor accept a seeming truth by virtue of its longevity alone; neither accept as a truth the false made appealing by the cosmetics of spectacle nor reject a truth obscured by the cosmetics of spectacle. The truth of things, which must be our concern always, is revealed through words rightly used and rightly taken. That revelation is the art of all liberal arts.

A brief word on the rhetorical mode I have used: I was invited to present the Younts Lectures at Erskine College on February 11, 1987. There were to be three: the first primarily to students, the second to faculty, the final one to these now joined by alumni and townspeople. In preparing the lectures, I had in mind the audience and audiences: as a whole and in its parts. In preparing the book version of those lectures, I have attempted to reduce the more obvious intrusions of their oral origins. (The actual lectures accommodated only a brief portion of what is here presented.) The oral mode is nevertheless in root and branch of the whole beyond the possibility of removing it, nor do I believe it even desirable. To attempt such would change the nature of the whole. Indeed, it seems to me that the order of address to distinguishable audiences serves well the essential concern of the whole— the rescue of community through a recovery of liberal arts as supportive of community. The final section, "The Quest for Community Ground," is a formal argument about the nature of community. It presents the position from which I set out as a person and is a conclusion to the implicit growth, development, and reflection upon fundamental principles which I hope my reader as discrete person may come to dwell upon.

Insofar as we are, in respect to our intellectual potential and heritage, each member in the large audience of mankind, I believe my individual reader will respond comfortably to my rhetorical mode, whose intention is to draw us gradually into a presence of minds larger than our lone, individual personhood. Thus I address my reader first as student, which each of us is insofar as we are rightly willed toward ourselves. Next as teacher, as each of us is willy-nilly insofar as we bear witness of ourselves. Then as member of community, in which proper relation we must, as intellectual creatures, continue active as both student and teacher. The final address is to the reader as that person who reflects upon his membership in community under all aspects of his citizenship in community.

In such a community of mind as I would celebrate, our experience of words may be to us as if we were actually in attendance on that February day when these present words, or some of them, were first said to a breathing audience. For when words are used with an ordinate respect, one hears them on a February 11, 1987, or October 31, 1988 (as I now set down these), or on the particular day on which one happens to turn these pages and encounter my voice in them, whatever the calendar occasion. For the mystery of words is that they always have presence in a present moment—the moment in which we hear them actually or hear them out of turned pages—whatever the surrounding accidents of history.

Marion Montgomery
All Saints' Eve, 1988

Liberal Arts and Community

I | Liberal Arts: The Sorting of Clichés

The simple believeth every word; but the prudent man looketh well to his going.
  —Proverbs 14:15

Although it may not appear to be true of me from the spectacle of an actual presence before you (such is vanity), though it may well be biographical fact called in question once I begin to speak, I have taught for more than thirty years. Nevertheless, I am quite aware that one of the more insidious fallacies of mind is that longevity signifies wisdom and truth. Whether my thirty years have led me into the country of wisdom is the very point at issue here—with you cast as student and cast as well as juror whether you want to be or not. It is only slightly reassuring to us older, if not wiser, men that it was ever thus. Forever and a day, wise age has addressed hopeful youth, always most poignantly. Remember with me an ancient scene. In the midst of the battle for Troy, King Nestor talks at length about the old battles—about the days when it was really rough—while the young warriors around him are struggling to hold their own against the fierce Trojans with whatever hopeful youth they can muster.

Young men, young scholars now themselves ancient, on one occasion at least attempted to prove Homer's great poem the product of several hands, in part on the basis of the seeming incongruity of language in this scene. In the scene, desperate action is afoot in a lively language of event, even as Nestor is maundering on and on about the good old days when warriors of his generation really had rough battles. It is as if he were talking around a campfire with young boy scouts rather than to bloody young men in the midst of battle. What an older and wiser scholar might remark of the seeming incongruity—so long as he is actively this side of senility, though at the same time safely beyond youth's anxious innocence—is that the great poet who makes our first great poem understands humanity in all its shadings. Especially he understands those varied foibles whereby we demonstrate our common if sometimes discomforting humanity. Homer knows both brash youth and tedious age and takes delight in the comedy that results from their being in each other's company, even in the midst of desperate battle.

But at least the young warriors in Homer had the relief from Nestor of arrows and spears raining down upon them. Such might be welcomed distraction from a Nestor's tediousness. Alas, your own best hope would seem to be the chapel bell, but it is a long way off. From the days of Nestor to your own, old men have maundered on about their youth and their father's youth. Since Homer, the young—impatient of their future—have struggled to seize the moment's advantage out of the lingering grasp of seemingly helpless old men.

Though I freely admit my inclination to tediousness through high sentence, I declare as well on behalf of all old Nestors a genuine concern that you might not greenly or foolishly be indifferent to any wisdom that might be buried somewhere in an old man's words. Though I sound like Nestor or Polonius to you, I profess (since I am by calling a professor) that I am at least still young enough to have confidence in supple, green youth. I believe you capable of separating sanity from senility, though you will not have experienced either fully as yet. To separate sense from nonsense is not a power reserved to youth or age. At the same time, that is an exercise less exciting no doubt than dodging Trojan arrows, even though a failure there may be as deadly to you as any literal shaft in the rib cage. Not that I expect you to believe me—at once. But at least entertain the possibility; at worst such occupation might help while away the minutes till the bell sound.

My own innocent confidence in you springs from an ancient faith that we are each given possibilities of heart and mind sufficient to discover the truth of things. I also know, out of my thirty years' war, that you are not likely to have perfected those gifts of both heart and mind toward an abidingly safe sanity. The evidence abounds that you are all too susceptible to the machinations of words. Through words, wily old and young men sometimes confound bright youth and confident age. At every hand is evidence thereof, if one pause quietly out of the slings and arrows or this side the chapel bell. Through words falsely taken we come to embrace academic or political or social programs that are suspect once we counter false words with rigorous thought. At the immediate sensual local level, we know how one may be led to choose one drink or insurance policy or soap or brand of blue jeans over another. Ultimately through our own use of words, we come to be what we are in the world, for good or bad.

And so I come to my principal theme and song: the decisive importance of words rightly taken to any perfection of one's heart and mind. A refrain to that song: Through the concert of heart and mind tuned by true words, we may move beyond our individual, separate aspirations and become aware that we hold humanity in common; so then we have a common—that is, a community—responsibility to words. We begin to understand, for instance, what St. Paul means when he says that we are members one of another. It is through words, through the signs we make one to another, that we discover ourselves bound one to another in a community larger than our private selves, larger than our lives taken only individually and independent of other lives. To realize this importance in our words may lead us to examine more closely such a word as I have just used, a word I wish to use with as much resonant wisdom as I can summon. The word I mean is *bound*.

To bind; to be bound: a richly suggestive term, since we use it so variously. Within the variety of use lie all the hazard and joy of our becoming, all the prospect of our becoming what it is allowed that we may become. The moment we begin to look closely at our words, we see not only deeper into the words themselves, that community gift that is ours for the taking; we also begin to see more deeply into ourselves, into our possibilities. My temptation here is to dwell too long on this chosen word, so rich it is. But there are others we must come to, and so we must touch on it but lightly.

To begin, we remember that old Southern hymn that says "I'm bound for the Promised Land." That line is thick with the history of our journey westward: the ancient passage out of Egypt into Canaan, all the way through time and space down to those wayfarers who settled New England with their own settled conviction of having come to a New Canaan. With a slight shift in the syntax, we discover the word *bound* is more complex than its apparent form, the letters and segments of words that make a word. If I say "I am bound *by* the Promised Land," more is changed than a prepositional phrase. The verb *bound* itself suddenly changes its burden. When we take refuge in the dictionary, what we discover is that, despite the literal identity of the verb in each sentence, *to be bound by* and *to be bound for* are quite different ideas, the verbs themselves having quite different histories. *To be bound for home* and *to be bound by home* say radically different things about one's relation to home, to those with ears to hear. It is just such radical differences that give the foreign student difficulty with our language—as we should have similar difficulties with his native language. There is a particular blessing in being born into a language, whatever language it is. But what most troubles me is that we increasingly abuse this native gift; even a recourse to the dictionary we tend to object to—it is a seeming imposition upon us, the more so when we have through carelessness abandoned the heritage of the language given us. That abandonment, charged to you as students by your diligent teachers, is actually a failure to be laid at the feet of all our community who meet in that language, your teachers (I include myself) no less than parents or neighbors. One comes to have ears to hear from long listening, from reflecting on the depths in such sounds, where meaning settles and accumulates. Meaning is to be summoned out of that sound to be used by the mind in quieting the heart's restlessness. Developing one's ear and tongue to value meaning is what we call education. But one becomes educated, not only in a concert of his own mind and heart through words, but through that larger concert of members in the body of community, one's teachers and parents and neighbors and media gurus and politicos. Because most of these do not, in fact, accept the responsibility for words as the community's inheritance, it makes your own responsibility the more difficult, makes it even more a responsibility, one with a moral obligation attached by your very act of professing to be a student.

To bind. There is that other old hymn that says, "Blest be the tie that binds." We say, in self-justification, "I am bound to do thus and so." Or we say judgmentally, "It was bound to happen to her, to him." We bind stocks of wheat—or used to. We know, at

THE SORTING OF CLICHÉS | 5

any rate, that superglue binds metal or wood. In New Zealand (September 1986) a prisoner used superglue to bind his hand with his visiting wife's, so that they could stay together. (A hospital staff parted them.) We feel ourselves bound in love to our family, to our hometown, to certain ideas—and less solubly than by superglue. We even get into a bind when we have not done those things which we ought to have done—have not finished the last act of *Hamlet* or done the algebra or history assignment. Sometimes, when we have done those things we ought not to have done, we may even in extremities be bound over by a grand jury, bound for more concrete bonds than we might wish.

When we discover such profuse presences in what seems but one simple little group of letters, our heart bounds with anxiety or joy, for we know that words do indeed touch realities, especially the realities of our own relation to a world larger than the self. We may long for some bound to the risks that words put us to. We may be tempted to put off all restraint, free ourselves of the bonds of mind in words, and be content with drumbeats on the loud stereo. We say, "Let who will bind himself to the education of the mind and heart; I shall feel my way through the pulse in my wrist." Still, we feel compelled to *say* this, to use words in justifying abandoning our responsibility for words. So long as we do so, all is not lost. On the other hand, responding to sound without meaning, the stereo drumbeat, will make of us only an extension of pulse, living by impulse. And I must tell you that even ferns are wiser than that. I have in mind the experiments made in which plants are subjected first to Mozart and then to Rock 'n' Roll. It is a measurable effect that in the first instance the plants lean toward the music as they prosper, while in the second they gradually wither away from the sound. One suspects that the plants themselves are responding to a meaning in the music, not simply to sound at the level of physics, since volume doesn't seem to be the determinant. At any rate, there is quite possibly a meaning in the experiment that encourages parents at least to believe there to be virtue in their own reaction to loud music. Meanwhile, their children, with less wit than desperation, are likely to mutter about their moss-grown elders.

In such words lie the possibilities of our understanding ourselves and the world, requiring our careful analysis of such experiments as these measuring plants' reactions to music. Words, the one property we hold in common, whose value fluctuates in response to our common use or abuse of them. Even so, we shy from words, in part because they are themselves. They seem to have an existence independent of our uses; words are wild, intractable, unwilling to be vaguely valued and used. They seem delighted to take part in that comic exercise whereby we put our foot in our mouths, as we say. Indeed, as the French philosopher Brice Parain remarks in his little book *A Metaphysics of Language,* words seem actively subversive. If you have recently tried to deal with the words in a sonnet by Gerard Manley Hopkins or the mysteries of such a word as $E=MC^2$, you will at once no doubt sympathize with Parain when he says, "That which lasts best, apart from the sun, . . . is words. The first words that were collected have succeeded in preserving their meaning even after the fall of the empires in which their language was spoken. What is revealed to us then in our moments of silence is that we are a kind of compost heap on which language germinates, grows, and flowers." And again, "We might well wonder if language does not nourish itself on our existence as a tree in the forest lives on dead leaves." Out of that climate of fear, we may well conclude that the college or university is peopled by strange creatures who were once perhaps men and women but who now are enslaved to words, having mutated through strange radiations from words. They seem rather strange fanatics, consumed by a mystery in signs that seem to us of more importance to the signs than to ourselves. These strange creatures, called faculty, seem quite ready to let a student's blood when he places even a comma in the wrong place or fails the details of his fruit fly lab experiment, the laboratory being another species of commitment to words. Strange creatures indeed—these faculty—whom we as students are expected to honor and obey, though it is only with great difficulty that we may love them. They are, after all, more tedious than King Nestor.

Thank God for dictionaries, then? For so long as we have individual words incarcerated, safely straitjacketed by precise definition, they may be under control. We may then the more comfortably ignore them since they are safely jailed. We may even be grateful for those penal reservations, the dictionaries, where words are removed from the world—a world we sometimes even speak of as the "real world." We are particularly grateful for those colleges which serve as holding stations of words. So long as words are *in* the dictionary, or used *in* the colleges with due attention to their ordering, we may feel reasonably safe from their threats of subversion. If they are not law-abiding citizens of the real world, at least there is some restraint upon them brought by official guardians. And their probation officers, the teachers on the campus compound, keep a watchful eye on them, freeing one's own eyes for the "real world." If we can't command them, at least Sam Johnson or Noah Webster or a committee using computers can. For the dictionary at least asserts that words are properly the instruments of mind and not mind the slave of words. If pressed for illustration of the mind's commanding use of them, their guardians may even supply us with resonant names like Plato and St. Thomas Aquinas and Einstein and Newton.

If only such an attitude were safely valid, one might leave words to the control of dictionaries and committees, even perhaps in desperation to Professors of English. But, short of an individual's consent to absolute silence and the absence of all gestures—including the pounding foot in sync with drumbeats—we continue in a world where words more nearly besiege dictionaries and professors than submit to being ordered by such instruments and used for community. With a touch of terror, we realize that even with precise definition—the word shorn of the liveliness of context and confined to its history by alphabetical entry—we are yet dependent, both committee and professor, upon mercenary words. So we are always breaking them out of stir to use in the moment's crisis, only to have them turn on us as likely as not. In our day, the jail-keepers are among the first taken hostage, having too carelessly treated words as trustees, confident of exercising control through the laws of logic and the instruments of science. How disturbing always to discover that laws and instruments alike turn out to be the subjects of words.

If one ventures too far upon such thoughts about words, he gains some glimmer of sympathy for the medieval Scholastic. One might even by intuition, if not through words, sense that the old question of the number of angels on the head of a pin is a concern for the problem of words rather than a concern for angels or pins per se. To make such a discovery and then to turn to the current concerns of particle physics is to discover just how much ours too is a Scholastic age, in the formal sense of that phrase. For the most central problem in particle physics at the moment is a control of language toward penetrating the secrets of elemental being. The problem posed increasingly to the scientific mind, if my reading of the weekly issues of *Science News* is at all dependable, is the necessity of a metaphysical understanding of physical phenomena. Because of the seeming necessity of touching reality beyond the senses and even beyond our most subtle machines, words only promise to reveal phenomena— words themselves governing suppositions about being, about existence. Those words, derived from the subtle language of mathematics, are focused vaguely through sophisticated machinery which repeatedly proves too gross for reality itself. Only a metaphysical vision would seem to promise any rescue, a most horrible conclusion that is being forced upon many scientific minds yet living in nineteenth-century mechanistic surety. The particle physicist increasingly sounds like the theologian. The astronomer, or at least one of them, feels it necessary to say, though affirming himself agnostic,

The religious faith of the scientist is violated by the discovery that the world had a beginning under conditions in which the known laws of physics are not valid, and as a product of forces or circumstances we cannot discover. . . . For the scientist who has lived by his faith in the power of reason, the story ends like a bad dream. He has scaled the mountains of ignorance; he is about to conquer the highest peak; as he pulls himself over the final rock, he is greeted by a band of theologians who have been sitting there for centuries.

So Robert Jastrow, professor of astronomy and geology at Columbia University, ends his *God and the Astronomers*.

If physicists and astronomers who have been rather comfortably resigned to atheism or agnosticism are increasingly sounding like theologians and philosophers, they do so out of necessities in what words have to say about the implications of reality, even when reluctant colleagues may find such inclinations less than "scientific." Such a shift, I imply, is heretical to the nineteenth-century scientific mind, dominant among us but itself entrapped by history. A few, a remnant, find themselves otherwise committed, believing with Socrates that it is better to know than not to know, perhaps even believing at last with St. Thomas that knowing the truth of things is the ultimate end of reason, even when the truth of things requires an admission that things *are* because they are *created*.

In pursuit of this high calling of reason there has come into formal existence, at Berkeley, California, a Center for Theology and the Natural Sciences, a modest enough beginning toward metaphysical vision. At a recent conference the members engaged in a critique of "Critical Realism in Science and Religion," discussing the relation of quantum mechanics to pantheism, atheism, Eastern Orthodoxy, and western orthodoxy. Critical realism, incidentally, is that doctrine which proposes that science is saying "something real about the nature of things" (*Science News,* April 26, 1986). That proposition, as was observed by a participating scholar trained in Scholastic thought, raises the most ancient of questions: whether scientific theories indeed say something about the nature of things in a limited correlation of statement to reality, or whether such theories are only theories concerned with "saving the appearances," that ancient formulation of scientific intent which we inherit from Plato and Aristotle. "Saving the appearances" is a necessary compromise between our desire for absolute authority of reason and the finitude of mind. (One might find Owen Barfield's engaging words in *Saving the Appearances: A Study in Idolatry* most revealing on this controversy.)

The "antirealists" at the conference, descendants of Descartes and of the Nominalists, argued that physics makes problems for such a fundamentalist creed as scientific "critical realism." One of the participants, illustrating his argument with mechanics, asserts a relativism in which one denies the necessity of one answer to every question, which is the position of one given to "saving the appearances." The difficulty of this relativistic response, however, is that it is not content to rest its necessity on the finiteness of man's mind, on the impossibility of so refining words that they encompass reality. If that were possible, we should then be able to rest in a fulfillment of mind, knowing all that can be known. This particular respondent insists rather that any statement about the nature of things in fact says nothing "real" about things. The point becomes certain when he insists that, in quantum mechanics, there are no paradoxes.

Science News's excellent reporter of the conference, D. E. Thomsen, remarks this a conclusion that will amaze most physicists. For as he says, "To most physicists the conjunction of particle and wave natures in a single being is as close to an antithesis as you are likely to get." He alludes to the most conspicuous "being" in which this antithesis coincides, light, upon which all physicists have come to depend in a very fundamentalist way since Einstein. And I mean fundamentalist here in a religious sense. For our purposes, let us note that the physicist, and most especially the particle physicist, is religiously (that is, through faith and hope) committed to the revelation in words, since all his instruments are too crude and primitive to resolve the paradox that light is both wave and particle. What dawns upon him is that to deny paradox in his words is to deny both the mystery in things and the precision in words, so that he becomes speechless being, equipped with inadequate instrument. Some of those philosophers and theologians who have been waiting on the mountaintop for the arrival of the scientist might well observe that the denial of paradox through an arbitrary relativism, whose authority is merely the mind of the relativist himself, is a most curious position for reason to take. If this mind is the ultimate authority over questions of reality, over the relation of words to the truth of things, then no further conversation about the truth of things is possible. Words will have achieved at last the ultimate freedom of anarchy, a final fragmentation of community more destructive to mankind than those fearsome bombs we credit Einstein's physics with. We might observe in passing that those bombs seem an adequate proof that relativism is not absolute, that words engaging the truth of things is precisely the combination that brings such bombs into the community. And they do "work"—those bombs.

Rather certainly Einstein himself would reject such relativism, believing that "the scientist is possessed by the sense of universal causation." For the pure relativistic position has implicit in it a solipsism so rigorous that each mind must at last declare itself the only world that exists, though we may well wonder to whom or to what it makes such declaration. Here surely is a contradiction, not a paradox. That question is seldom posed, since it is a first step in discovering that relativism is an inadequate faith to live by. To *declare* at all, of course, requires the use of one's anarchist words, which in an offense to solipsism turn their faces toward an outer world. Thus an inescapable contradiction in the antirealist's position as he engages the realist: As he insists on the purity of his relativism, he already violates it by his consent to engage a mind not his own. He does so through absolutist words which, insofar as he orders them persuasively in relation to his perceptions about quantum physics, imply the existence of beings beyond the words, and of truths to be spoken to and of those beings. At the simplest level, he acknowledges the existence of the critical realist. He is in a position not unlike that of the art-for-art's-sake purist poet who, concerned only with his inviolable poem, nevertheless sends it to the poetry editor at the *New Yorker*.

Now, I do not pretend that what I have been saying about the new Scholasticism of particle physics—about the "critical realist" and the "antirealist"—is immediately available to you as I talk, any more than I pretend to be an expert in this Scholastic physics. But what I hope you will see at once is the heavy dependence, in this very crucial argument, upon words held in common by those who are arguing, words including the most abstruse symbols of mathematics in this particular argument. I would hope that in addition you might notice analogies between such seemingly esoteric concerns in particle physics and your own daily encounters with the world. Such arguments affect us more immediately than we sometimes acknowledge. Consider, for instance, the differences in technology at this moment and in 1905, when Einstein galvanized us as a new age by suggesting that $E=MC^2$.

And you might as well consider this parallel: The battle waged between the critical realists and antirealists at the California conference bears rather striking similarities to the current and conspicuous battle between the religious Fundamentalists and their Modernist brothers. Incidentally, the Modernists have recently discovered the rhetorical—and hence the political—advantage of declaring themselves "moderates," perhaps trading on the residual authority of our Greek inheritance, particularly that from Aristotle's argument that virtue is a mean between two extremes. The advantage here is a seeming reasonableness of the position without the complication of absolutes in regard to virtue or to truth. With an Aristotelean mean so adapted, one can defer questions of transcendence—for a time. The scientific fundamentalists we have been talking about, the critical realists, when they consider light under the dual aspect of particle and wave, are dealing with mystery analogous to the mystery of the soul's relation to the body, a paradoxical conjunction in the single being "as close to an antithesis as you are likely to get." Plato discovered this paradox in being, in existence, most eloquently in words, and so we have struggled with it ever since. The extreme factions in this struggle are those critical realists the Manicheans on the one hand and the antirealists who deny soul's existence on the other. These, however, are not the only alternatives in the paradox. They are only the most spectacular simplifiers of the mystery which, in various versions, has been with us at least since Plato and Democritus, and more probably since Adam sat down at evening after laboring in the earth all day and looked up at the stars, before Eve called him to his porridge.

I have quite deliberately introduced ideas that are confusing, baffling, disturbing, even as they are insistent and exciting to the mind. They are ideas as ancient as the Ionian physicists and as recent as our last class in literature or mathematics or biology. And they are all ideas available, in their gross or refined presences to the mind, only through signs—only through words of one sort or another, whether sprung from our own present thought or encountered as sign-held thought by Plato or Einstein. To fear the complexity of words—either because they might reveal to us that a treasured "reality" is proved at last merely an illusion we hold on to sentimentally, or because words through their treachery may distort actual reality—that is to become hopelessly lost, victims sacrificed to the very words one fears. In the "real world," it leaves one, by analogy once more, in the condition of the hopelessly poor or the displaced beggar. One is left dependent upon minds not his own and so he is susceptible to the abuse of random intellectual charity from others. I use *displaced* person in the analogy for this reason: I suspect that this necessary labor with words, undertaken with fear and trembling, is the most fundamental inheritance we have from our first displaced person, Adam; the necessity of bearing witness to truth through words is the principal consequence of Original Sin. One making his way through the world by the sweat of his brow raises that sweat in more ways than by digging potatoes.

But one need not agree with me on a Christian doctrine to recognize just how crucial words are to the life that he would save, namely his own. Without words a great silence falls on our hearts and minds, the silence of death itself as we pass backward through the stages of our life to animal and then perhaps into automaton existence. To refuse the engagement with words is a gradual suicide of mind. To choose silence over the struggle with words in this manner is to choose an unearned silence; at its best, such a silence leaves us in the panic of isolation from all else but our own flickering, guttering consciousness. Eventually it leads to a separation of consciousness itself into parts in an endless interior dialogue of the fragmented self. Without words, the world is empty; without words, we discover ourselves empty and try to force our existence by dividing our self so that it may at least converse with itself. Psychiatrists might, indeed, remark the desert soul in such division and go beyond the merely biochemical imbalances that occupy that discipline at the moment.

So then, what of the paradox that our philosopher Brice Parain remarks: Without words we are nought; with words we are but fodder to the ravenous fungus of words. With our use of words, we have said, we risk losing our lives, assuming that we take life to be something more than Newtonian mechanical forces or Darwinian accidental animal mechanism. The risk lies, as Parain suggests in *A Metaphysics of Language,* in that we must distrust what we say, knowing that "each of our words [has] two faces—one turned toward being that it represents, and the other toward the negation of being that it practices by not being what it represents." That is, the word *tree* is not the tree itself, and once we focus mind on the word *tree,* something seems to have gone out of the very tree we try to point to through the word.

This problem with language, which Parain engages so dramatically, is the inevitable consequence of the Nominalist's separation of signs from creation. Insofar as one vests his faith in a reality of sign separated from creation, through which faith the gnostic mind would build its own world, the shock of reality will be inevitable and traumatic, for the separated signs must be turned back upon the separated creation if any new world is to be built. An encounter of Nominalist sign with actual existence calls the sign in question. Nominalism is inevitably eroded by the Nominalist's experience of reality, an inevitable experience since his actual existence is of and in the world and inseparable from the world, however much he struggles to disengage his signs. Words (signs) lack integrity when separated from creation. But still, they are inadequate to it, even when there is an active mind engaging word with reality. *Tree* is always inadequate to the reality of a tree, no matter how heavy the modifiers we add to *tree* in an attempt to catch the reality. Hence a perversity in words when one vests faith in words as comprehensive of reality. St. Thomas, in opposition to the Nominalist William of Occam, insisted that words cannot contain—comprehend—reality and so are subservient to reality. Occam, by separating words, sought an absolutist power in word. But the relation of word to reality is one made in heaven, or more accurately or immediately, intrinsic to the created nature of man himself, not easily divorced by man's intellect.

If words do not comprehend, neither do they kill, reality, except that reality of the intellect which by its consent to the absolute separation of sign from the thing signified attempts to vest its own authority over being in the sign itself. I have intended to suggest that modern science is haunted by its consent to such a separation. As science approaches a necessity of acknowledging a transcendent which limits infinity, as increasingly in our day it seems forced to do, its confidence in its own absolutist domination of sign is increasingly shaken. Nearing its limit in infinity, science finds its faith in finitude shaken. If it were otherwise in this relation of sign to signified, we could be comfortable with names only, as young Stephen Dedalus thinks himself capable of being as artist in James Joyce's *Portrait of the Artist as a Young Man*. Stephen would make a world of words, rising aloof from his own word-made world in a divine indifference. But though clever, Stephen is fatuous as artist, as Joyce was painfully aware. Stephen's words at last become not simply cryptic but fragmentary as he declines into an arrogant separation from the created world that has sustained him all along.

If words were commensurate with existence—if *tree* encompassed, comprehended, the actual tree—we could either live in a world separate from actual trees, as Stephen fatuously supposes, or we could with impunity abandon all names, needing neither verbs nor participles nor coordinate and subordinate conjunctions. Neither would we then need quantum mechanics, or biology, or any branch of science. We should no longer need the humanities. Most assuredly we should not have a need of colleges, especially liberal arts colleges. We would then either reject the world, needing only names; or reject the words, needing only things. But in the beginning was that Word, which is the cause of creation, and if creation inevitably punctures Stephen Dedalus' balloon of words, bringing him crashing into reality, those who on the other hand would abandon words must begin to stumble toward words again. We must do so, even if less spectacularly recalled to the complexity of existence than is that arrogant young Stephen, whose motto as artist, let us not forget, is Lucifer's: I will not serve.

Perhaps the wordless might stumble awkwardly under the guidance of those radical antinominalists that Gulliver encounters in his travels. At Jonathan Swift's Legado Academy, the learned doctors thereof solve this problem of words in relation to reality. Gulliver reports the matter as follows: "An expedient was therefore offered, that since Words are only the Names of Things, it would be more convenient for all Men to carry about them, such Things as were necessary to express the particular Business they are to discourse on." Gulliver, with his usual innocent enthusiasm, reports seeing some of these scholars accompanied by servants carrying great bags of things; when they stop to converse with each other, they open the bags and hold up objects to each other. Their "conversation" over, the objects are stored in the bags, the servants hoist bags on shoulders, and the scholars' progress continues. Such is the basis of a universal language, since it would be "understood in all civilized nations, whose goods and utensils are generally of the same kind or nearly resembling. . . . And thus ambassadors would be qualified to treat with foreign princes or ministers of state to whose tongues they were utter strangers."

Ambassadors would have no need of a common word, since the things would suffice. Of course the absurdity is self-evident but might be heightened. We might suppose the complication of the several callings of community. Carpenters would have one sort of baggage of things, bakers and butchers another. But what happens when carpenter attempts to buy bread or meat, being able to talk only with his saw and hammer? When we have imagined a Chaucerian comedy in such exchanges, undoubtedly ending in a fight between the carpenter with his hammer and the baker with his oven's hot coals, we might consider how like this is to our own treatment of specialized words as things: how difficult it is for, say, the professional educationist to communicate with the local members of the PTA, or the neurosurgeon with the patient about to go under the knife, which is now more likely to be a laser beam. Words having become not only things themselves, independent of other things and separated into specializations within their own thingness, community must increasingly fragment.

A corollary to this invention of language as natural things at Swift's Legado Academy, advanced and permeating our world since Swift's day and bearing directly upon specialized words as things (by doctors or educationists or physicists), is the *fact* as a thing declared into being out of eighteenth-century rationalism. A fact is a portion of mysterious existence abstracted and sterilized by contraction from existence; in its most usual manifestation in the affairs of our society, we encounter it in tables of statistics. The reality of our nation, for instance, is the *facts* of the latest census. Ralph Waldo Emerson provides the text for such reductionism. "Our life," he says, "is indeed nothing but an endless procession of facts." Again, "A fact is an Epiphany of God." But then God has little presence in Emersonian thought, since "the world is nothing, the man is all," including man's being his own divinity. Hence, "on every fact of his life [man] should rear a temple of wonder and joy" to his own divinity. Of course, Emerson is as fatuous as Joyce's young Stephen, though his arguments have permeated the intellectual community, especially as that community is found established in the community's much-honored academy. With such thinkers as Emerson, one has no need of Swift's Legado Academy.

If this seems an excessive objection to facts, it is prompted by the excessive devotion to them which runs through the whole of our community existence. Note how such Emersonian worship of denatured nature touches your own activities, including recreation. The most popular manifestation of fact as icon is revealed by the popularity of the game called Trivial Pursuit; the term *trivia* nevertheless acknowledges that fact may indeed have its limits. From my own Legado Academy, I have an announcement of a course, given for academic credit, open to all students and requiring "no prerequisites," ignorance thus advertised as virtue in the announcement. It is called "A History of American Radio &

Television," but what it promises the student is, and I quote, **"A COLLEGE COURSE IN TRIVIA."** The fine print promises more substance than the come-on phrase, a concession to the scattering of academic fundamentalists still surviving, but it intends to capitalize, in the economic sense, on the current hunger for the trivialization of intellect.

If you have a sense of a higher calling for the mind than its being a repository for trivia, there is hope not only for you but for the community whose life is your responsibility. But always confronting you will be the temptation to the silence of refusal, especially given such a disoriented age as you are privileged to participate in. I dare say each of us knows this temptation which, if exacerbated in our day, is nevertheless as old as Adam. It will have come upon you no doubt at some point when you sat down to write a freshman theme. I can assure you that one never quite moves beyond that temptation, which is to accept the silence of a refusal of life.

Now this silence of defeat is to be distinguished from a very valid silence, quite different from the gnawing desire for what would be an unearned silence. I myself must contend with the corrosive species of silence, even after my thirty years of wrestling words to try to make them signify something true and beautiful about existence, without at the same time letting them violate the complex reality of existence. My words to you at this very moment are evidence to my point. I would be much safer were I in Crawford, Georgia, talking to my fire, with logs stacked at hand against the chill.

As for that legitimate silence, I am equally confident that not many of us—even the most ancient among us—come fully to enjoy it in this world. St. Thomas Aquinas speaks of this wise silence when, near the end of his life, looking at the great monuments of unaging intellect he had himself constructed with words, he declared them as straw in the light of his fuller vision of reality. He put down his quill, closed his book, and wrote no more. Not senility in St. Thomas, though that would be a convenient conclusion to some, but a wisdom earned through an arduous journey of mind through the aid of words. Of that silence, St. Thomas remarks: "It is therefore said of us that when we come to the end of our knowledge, we acknowledge God as the Unknown, because the mind has made most progress in understanding when it recognizes that God's essence lies beyond anything that the mind in its state of being-on-the-way can comprehend." And so, "God is honored by silence—not because we cannot say or understand anything about Him, but because we know that we are incapable of comprehending Him."

My concern is not to convert you immediately to this high silence of honoring God to which St. Thomas comes at last, though I pray you may arrive at that state of mind in consequence of your journey, your own "being-on-the-way." Quite the contrary, I am urging the necessity of that journey accompanied at every step by those unruly creatures, words. You must be brave enough to release them from their incarceration in ink and then strong enough to command them, if you are to do anything more than wander idle in the desert of your own mind. To turn in a blank paper at a final examination means one thing, if by this statement we mean a final examination at the end of a course in algebra or history. It means something quite other if we are speaking metaphorically of St. Thomas' final examination before the incomprehensible God. That, I have often said to students, is *the* final examination, to which one comes through courage and strength and hope, under the enveloping auspices of grace.

And so there is no release for you now. The freedom that the assembly bell promises is an illusion, for at once you must either exchange words with your friends about this strange mouthing of an old man—or avoid such exchange with your conscience an unwelcomed irritant. Believe me, you are much safer now sitting there than you will be out there in the "real world." Out there, you are bound, whether you will or no, to order words in relation to the truth of things as you encounter them. I hope that by your consent to words you will realize yourself at risk but not be afraid. For when the self is not at risk, it is either in a state of beatitude— an unlikely prospect by the end of this talk for any of us here assembled—or the self is dead or at the least very gravely ill.

Slowly we discover that, whereas we are bound to make our own way in a journey of mind, we are also already bound by the journeys others have made before us: we are bound no less by those surrogate fathers we each have—often without knowing we have them. Einstein, we suggested, fathered an Age, and we are the children of that age and grandchildren of Einstein, whether we might wish to be or not. We are directly descended from Plato and Aristotle, from Francis Bacon and John Locke, from Descartes and Kant, from Edmund Burke and Rousseau, from Shakespeare and Keats, from Emerson and Nathaniel Hawthorne. So the immediate practical necessity to our education is the discovery of our hidden parentage, lest we continue intellectual orphans. A liberal arts education provides the means for your discovering your lineage, the opportunity for you to winnow your inheritance. The only sieve suitable to this recovery of your inheritance of an essential past is words, words, words.

In sorting the nuances of our fathers' words, we come to discover the limits of our own being, the range of our freedom to become, the bounds of the journey we are to make. If we can discover that in being bound by our fathers, we are not thereby immobilized by them—if we can discover that even the freedom of our supposed innocence with words (which is sometimes described as wild youth) is a gift we receive at risk from our fathers—we may come to a maturity of a continuing freedom. That is, we may understand freedom as limited by the very gifts of our existence, not only by our biological inheritance or social or economic, but by the intellectual behest of those who came before us. Thus only can we reach an accommodation with our limits, accepting the inescapable reality that we are ourselves a given, within a given world, exercising given talents of heart and mind, body and soul. In fulfilling the gifts of our being, we reach the limits of freedom and accept those limits as themselves gifts no less than the freedom we exercise within them. Otherwise, we shall likely become very much like Hawthorne's Young Goodman Brown after his loss of innocent willfulness. We may live to be a hundred, but live as a "stern, a sad, a darkly meditative, a distrustful, if not desperate" soul, in whose name there shall be no hopeful verse carved on the tomb marking a final end.

The delicate shadings of reality, of the ways of our life and the life of the world—physically, mentally, spiritually—require our discovering those shades and bearing witness to the discovery. The shadings perceived in our finitude require our affirming an inheritance of truth and adding to the recovery of truth to both ourselves and to community. We are required to discard the false as well, the false we find in ourselves and others, including in our fathers no less than in our contemporaries or our children. In this respect, human life is judgmental action at every step; in witnessing, we judge. Even by drawing breath, we affirm; exhaling it, we may deny. Through accepting our bounden duty to words as the common holding of the community, we may at last command those words in an affirmation of life which is neither cynical nor merely a sentimental agitation of existence—our existence, our neighbor's, the world's. One may command with authority words anciently or currently abused, even when the words sound like barren clichés to those who as yet have no ears to hear.

For some of us, for instance, the words William Faulkner spoke in accepting the Nobel Prize for his fiction seem empty at best, facile in the cynic's coloring. For me at least, despite the spectacle of cliché, his words touch our lives at the point where we are bound to humanity from Homer down through Virgil's Rome and Shakespeare's England, to Hawthorne's New England and Faulkner's South. One must, says Faulkner, bear witness through words to "the old verities and truths of the heart, the old universal truths lacking which any story is ephemeral and doomed—love and honor and pity and pride and compassion and sacrifice." In accepting such bounden duty, with a deliberate activity of mind in support of those verities and truths of the heart, one begins to discover that most clichés—while seemingly empty, mouthed words—carry under their marred surfaces a coinage of that realm we call humanity. Indeed, they are the toll one pays for passage toward accepted ends, bringing one into his homeland, that community of members through which humanity is ordered and elevated.

Faulkner's cliché words might each require a lecture at least as long as this one to remove the residue of abuse that clings to them. To make such a recovery makes it possible for one to live with firm coinage spent but never exhausted; given but still possessed. One holds a phrase, which has been in and out of favor both with ourselves as individuals and ourselves collectively, a phrase that at moments seems to us nonsense but at other moments lights up our world. In a word's or phrase's high moment of light, reflected from the reality of the world, we may find ourselves ushered for a heartbeat into a country of high silence, a moment of vision. For me such a talisman, in a collect for peace from our Elizabethan prayer book, pleads to a God "whose service is perfect freedom." In that phrase, *service* means to convey an absolute binding of the self to God, through which paradoxically one possesses a perfect freedom. In perfect freedom one reaches the bounds of individual being, the limits of one's gifts of existence and callings. In such vision, though old, one discovers himself yet a joyful Young Goodman Brown. And being so bound, one enters the more fully into those inherited clichés, spends them with authority—which is to say, one uses them with the fullness of understanding whereby they become good angel to our actions rather than subversive of any significant action. At last then one may sing with full-throated ease, "Blest be the tie that binds."

No doubt you are getting restive. Not only have I been playing with words such as *bind,* but increasingly in that playfulness I have lured you nearer and nearer toward theological concerns— the principal no-no of our academic world. But those are the ultimate concerns, I would insist. At every point they are contingent upon our actions of mind in the world. I am not concerned to lure you into that country of an ultimate engagement here; I am intending only to forewarn you of that inevitability, one of the more irritating attitudes of age to youth. Actually, I am more concerned with your actions of mind within the world of the academy, believing full well the other will follow insofar as you become active intelligences. The impinging theological and philosophical concerns will come into your individual focus on their own, since they are everywhere you look, and insistent upon mind. Or, to put the matter in another metaphor, they are bound to do so because of the binding of existence by the Cause of existence. We are forced to philosophical questions.

Those concerns we may defer, though not avoid, trusting their fullest presence to be insistent to you as you approach the borders of an earned silence. What is more pressing, here and now, is your necessary preparation for the journey toward an encounter with ultimate questions. T. S. Eliot remarks his own progress, imitating in his poetry the actions of our common nature that place us on the way to the encounter. Of this common journey he says that each step of the way

> Is a new beginning, a raid on the inarticulate
> With shabby equipment always deteriorating
> In the general mess of imprecision of feeling,
> Undisciplined squads of emotion.

That shabby equipment is, of course, words—worn out by the constant friction of feeling and emotion from within us. For our traveling boots, which seem worn down only by the rocks and gravel of the trail—worn down from the outside—are also being worn from within, by our insistent feet. Never so conspicuously, so spectacularly, evident to us as the worn heel. But then we might notice how uneven the outer wear, a consequence of the way we each walk, the way we carry our weight in the world. And that is surely an influence from within. So Eliot, looking back after his own impressive journey as poet, examining his worn boots at a rest stop, laments his twenty years as "largely wasted" in "Trying to learn to use words." These are the years of "Prufrock" and "The Waste Land" and "Ash-Wednesday," hardly wasted words most of us would say. What he knows and declares, however, is that his and our

> Words strain,
> Crack and sometimes break, under the burden,
> Under the tension, slip, slide, perish,
> Decay with imprecision, will not stay in place,

and above all else, "Will not stay still." For there is no rest for words under the pressure of our feelings and emotions as we try to make a way toward knowledge with our minds, toward seeing St. Thomas' "truth of things."

What Eliot, one of your and my fathers, would wish to encourage in us is that we, in this present, see to our equipment, which even at its best is already shabby and worn and bound to become more so until we may at last discard it to walk naked into a silence earned by our journeying. Such, surely, is the point of your being here, in this training camp set aside specifically for the gathering and repair of equipment for the most serious leg of your journeying. Those who bind you to this training—you by your consent foremost, and then your parents and teachers and neighbors—pray for you (as you must for yourselves) a sound preparation for the joyful perils that wait: after the chapel bell, after the examination in history or literature or mathematics, after the certifying of your equipment by the state patrol of mind—that is, after your diploma, duly signed by your president, is in your hand, authorizing and certifying your mind to go a-journeying. Insofar as those inspectors and certifiers understand the journey ahead to involve you—body, mind, and spirit—and its progress to be toward a unity of witness, then all manner of thing shall be well, to borrow from Mr. Eliot and Dame Julian of Norwich on the point. Such are the principles governing what we still call a liberal arts education, though its advocates unfortunately tend to defend that education on the low ground of pragmatic advantage to community—which is to say on the ground of mechanical convenience.

If the mind is trained to the end that it may conduct the body in comfort to a final inglorious rest, the community of humanity is in serious difficulty. Alas, I must tell you that such is the primary end, the principal emphasis of, most American academies, an emphasis under the rubric of *professionalism*. By *professionalism* is generally meant a specialized training toward a job in the marketplace—in business or government. Unless our concern for professionalism is leavened by the deeper and wider meanings in that term—that is, unless the word is used as more than a convenient cliché to sell materialistic success—we shall be led inevitably to the mind's ultimate service to the body, an enslavement intolerable to the gifts of our being. It will be so, even when we manage to disguise that end from ourselves through words loosely used. If, for instance, we take it that the use of punctuation is a formal convenience unattached to substance (and the use of *formal* and *substance* here, while consistent with our popular sense of the terms, is in fact contradictory to the scholastic depths of the terms), we shall have liberal arts courses at the college level devoted to mechanics only. To the extent that the liberal arts survive in our larger institutions, they do so largely at this level. One takes English courses so that one can write a good report; one takes a scattering of history so that the diploma's formula will have touched, if only briefly, concerns of the mind inconvenient to the impatient demands of so-called professionalism.

But consider a recent event of considerable consequence to community—*community* here meaning the conduct of our nation as community. *Time*, in its usual clever way, reports the event under the title "Rallying Round a Comma Cause," thereby placing the concern as a comic one, much ado about nothing. At the Republican convention in Dallas in 1984, a considerable debate erupted over "one jot of punctuation," as *Time* phrases it. In the party's platform statement were to appear words stating that the party would "oppose any attempts to increase taxes, which would harm the recovery and reverse the trend to restoring control of the economy to individual Americans." As students in this way station, we need not be concerned with Republican or Democrat; the point is not partisan. The point is that to remove the comma here would change what is said in a radical way. It should be possible, even for *Time,* to see that historical, philosophical, political complexities ride on this very comma. It is consequently a jot of punctuation with which the political science teacher, the philosophy teacher, the history teacher have serious concern. That comma may not be left to the Freshman English teacher. For it makes considerable difference whether one means that *all* taxes harm economic recovery and are to be rejected or whether only those particular taxes which alone harm the recovery are to be rejected. To treat the concern here as if it were but a modern version of the problem of how many angels may stand on a pinpoint is an indictment, not of the question at issue, but of those who do not read the question at issue. It is, in short, a most resonant comma; the consequences of our rejecting it or endorsing it affect our lives and our children's lives, if only in a somewhat worldly way.

In a less restricted way, because of larger or deeper consequence to community, I have in hand a letter to a student newspaper. The writer protests an earlier student's defense of liberal arts as necessary to full professional training. The earlier letter held that a rediscovery of the virtues of Greek and Latin was especially important to that training. The letter of protest insists to the contrary that the "study of these languages is an elitist practice, which further focuses one's attention inwards to our cultural history and glorious traditions." This angry young man insists that "the best way to develop word power is to use language at every opportunity. We must think language, dream language and live language in order to develop as much of a command over it as possible." What one notices in the words just quoted is that their user is already victim to a randomness in them, even though he recognizes as well the importance of controlling them lest the words overwhelm the user. His is a cry against any abiding presence in words. What he doesn't recognize is that the binding permeates the very words he uses; consequently, his words run counter to what he intends. In short, he puts his foot in his mouth.

One notices, for instance, the confusion in him that supposes the study of Greek and Latin to be elitist in a political and social sense, *elitist* being one of those devil words convenient to radical egalitarians. To be elitist in a secular egalitarian age is like being sinful in a Christian age. Hence the use here is a deliberately manipulative one, though the user misses the self-destruction in such a use. When a user of the word, in such a context as ours, knows that he is abusing the word to gain support of argument through its residual social and political connotations, he is intent upon rousing the rabble. But it is still a manipulative word when used only in ignorance, as I think this young man does. He will not go behind his father's word to see what it really says. In consequence, in his use of the word he bears false witness. To use the wrong word or to use the word wrongly, whether in ignorance or with intent to deceive, is to bear false witness.

This point is so crucial to the life of your mind that I must put it to you again. One central commandment is "Thou shalt not bear false witness." A deliberate half-truth is a lie. An ignorant half-truth is a lie. A deliberate lie is the act of a scoundrel, to use a kinder term than called for. An ignorant lie is the act of a fool, to use a term perhaps a bit stronger than called for. But either a deliberate lie or an ignorant lie incapacitates one for responsible position as witness to the truth of things. Compounding the deliberate and the ignorant lie requires the striking of one's testimony, though the most significant concern at the borders of the country of earned silence, at the point of THE Final Examination, is the destruction worked upon the journeyman himself by false witness. I do not for an instant suggest that any of us, save the saints, manage to exorcise ignorance completely, nor that it is easy to rid ourselves of that native willfulness in us that tempts us to deliberately deceive. That is where we must recover old virtues, humility in especial. Whether we do so or not, John Milton suggests, the destruction by willful lie is limited. When Lucifer declares in Heaven, "I will not serve," and finds himself in Hell's exile as Satan, the great paradox becomes that the Cause of all causes turns even Satan's evil to good account. That is the central irony of Milton's poem, which becomes transformed into paradox as the poem concludes.

Our passionate young protestor against Greek and Latin, let us notice before we leave him, heightens his condemnation of Greek and Latin as disciplines for the journey by borrowing from what is at best a pseudopsychology, which he has somewhere absorbed, probably in a required undergraduate liberal arts course. Such study, he says, "focuses one's attention inwards to our cultural history and glorious traditions." From the general tone of the letter, apparent even in this excerpt, we understand that our young man thinks traditions anything but glorious, whereas the truth is that some are and some are not. The blindness revealed *through* these words is not *in* these words; he fails to see that cultural history permeates them. The phrase *focuses attention inwards,* for instance, is more beholden to Freudian and post-Freudian machinations of "attention" than I dare say the phrase's user knows.

When I speak of a language as permeated by tradition, bearing a presence of the past in this moment when we use language, I mean as always *language* in an inclusive sense. Language is not only words but all our cultural statements: our architecture, institutions, even our machines, from electric fans to word processors—all that language you spend your first two or three years discovering in liberal arts courses in art, literature, history, social studies, physics. By *language* I mean all those *common* artifacts, including ideas engraved in the mind no less than statues in public places—all those artifacts that orient us in a present moment. Now all those presences of the past can be denied only by a blind faith in a mystical present, a faith that the present is somehow freed of the past. It is assumed that such a denial must lead inevitably to a glorious future.* Whenever anyone speaks to you in a

---

*The celebration of the refurbished Statue of Liberty on July 4, 1986, is an event worth reflecting upon, in relation to the problem of language. The general spirit was that of the worship of an icon, an icon idea in which centers, but only seemingly centers, such a diversity of incommensurates as may not be reconciled by idea as image. One cannot forget the French connection here, remembering the terror attendant upon similar erection of icon to abstract ideas in the eighteenth century. There was, in the popular spirit of our occasion, a strong suggestion that America really begins in 1886, with the raising of the Statue of Liberty.

dismissive way about "glorious traditions," intending by irony or sarcasm to dismiss tradition through a sweeping tone, you may be confident he is worshipfully tuned to some "glorious future," a dream world in whose service he would entrap your mind by illusion.

The sound student will know that when one argues that any insight into history is necessarily inward—private and elitist—that person is bearing false witness. In the country of truth such an argument is not only ignorantly or deliberately wrong in itself, it is consequentially destructive of the very community for which such a speaker professes a concern. Such uses of words are necessarily a perversion of, or an attempted perversion of, reality. Our young man in his attack on liberal arts education as inward is, I fear, leading himself to an ultimate inwardness, leading himself to a provincialism of spirit quite contrary to what he believes he champions. If he prevails in community, the end will be a provincial community. His argument already reveals him enlisted in the cause of a provincialism which Allen Tate describes most tellingly, so that his words are worth hearing and rehearing. Tate, arguing for a regionalism, as opposed to provincialism, says

Regionalism is . . . limited in space but not in time. The provincial attitude is limited in time but not in space . . . [P]rovincialism is that state of mind in which regional men lose their origin in the past and its continuity into the present, and begin every day as if there had been no yesterday. . . . [W]hat a difference—and it is a difference between two worlds: the provincial world of the present, which sees in material welfare and legal justice the whole solution to the human problem; and the classical-Christian world, based upon regional consciousness, which held that

---

It is interesting that some of our blacks found the event less than satisfying, remembering how they came to these shores—not through Ellis Island. It is interesting as well that others, myself among them, are aware of the implicit eradication of history, especially the turbulent years between Andrew Jackson and 1872 (when the Fourteenth Amendment was repealed, a bargain with the South over franchise toward the election of 1876). A great deal of spectacle accompanied our celebration, under cover of which much history is swept under the waters of New York Harbor. A convenient distraction to any discomfort was provided by the quarrel over the commercialization of the statue, as if in the commercial imaging Liberty's name were taken in vain. In a similar way, the very real agonies of spirit in consequence of slavery, raised to the level of spectacle, have allowed us to ignore consequential issues other than slavery in the period between Jackson and Reconstruction.

honor, truth, imagination, human dignity, and limited acquisitiveness, could alone justify a social order however rich and efficient it might be.*

Our young protestor, a provincial mind in Tate's sense, has mistaken, has misunderstood, such complexities in words as those to which we have pointed in that richly ancient Anglo-Saxon world *bindan*. Our safe guardian, the dictionary, reveals the word "akin" to the Old High German *binton*, "to bind," as it is akin to the Greek *peisma*, "cable." Such cables are of steel, though outwardly frayed sometimes, in innocence of which our young man concludes his rejection of them—his rejection of the past—with a passionate demand that we, too, abandon the past. We are to study, instead of Greek and Latin, contemporary living languages—Japanese, Chinese, Russian, Indian. As if those languages were themselves sprung *ex nihilo*, if I may be forgiven a phrase from a "dead" language. He speaks, that is, as if those languages taken in themselves have no history and reflect no continuing community of mind more recent than the latest trade transaction. He treats those languages as if they were things in a sack to be used as were those things Swift's professors at the Legado Academy toted about with them. We should approach language in this provincial manner, so his argument runs, because "our future will rest on our ability to communicate with them [the speakers of those languages]." To explore the implications of the Japanese or Indian or Chinese attitude toward the nature of man would be a considerable undertaking, which one might begin perhaps by reading the historian Christopher Dawson's analysis of the metaphysical grounds of those peoples as revealed in their words. Otherwise, of course, the meaning of trade agreements is inevitably ambiguous, since the letter of the law or contract is dead until the spirit of the citizen or party to contract enters into the letter. Having made his argument, our young man signs his name and his calling: He is a graduate student in market research.

I do not want to be misunderstood as making fun of this very serious young man and his passionate concern, any more than I wish to be understood as rejecting the importance of laws and contracts. He demonstrates in a rather palpable way the destructions visited upon his mind by the very institution supposedly de-

*"The New Provincialism," *Virginia Quarterly Review* (April, 1945).

voted to recovering and enlarging his mind out of the provincial inclinations that are inherent in our nature. It is as if he has too easily been sold a bill of goods, has traded his mental birthright for a mess of market statistics. It is inevitable, then, that he exhibit a limited, provincial understanding of his own and of our humanity. To discover the kinships between the Greek and Old High German and Old English verb *to bind* at the least enlarges our community. It at least reveals to us the abiding nature of humanity, which to deny must leave us at last merely committed to a pragmatic calling to do market research, to sell things through words for a materialistic survival as community in the world. And even if one were content to exist at that level, it might be worth discovering through Homer, for instance, that Odysseus is an early Yankee trader; that in Hinduism is implicit a fatalistic acceptance of the world which rejects the world, a position of some pertinence to trading with Hindoos.

Our young passionate protestor, like most of us, has had his birthright stolen by the academy itself, in the interest of a professionalism that is but the shell of professionalism. For it can but be a shell, empty of significant life, if professionalism sets aside or does not recognize at all the abiding, the continuing presence of all humanity at each moment of history. Without that recognition we can at best be comfortable for a moment in the world, and only so long as the world itself is seen as merely a collection of things to be used. We shall find ourselves (individually and communally) given to much noise, sound, and fury signifying nothing—a species, in fact, of that unearned silence I warned against. When one finds his true profession, he will have found what others speak of as his true calling. It is a calling both within and ultimately beyond the world, a calling which rejects neither the world nor the beyond. In it is the recognition of and devotion to his particular gifts. Through that recognition alone is it possible to become a true member of that body humanity, within which and to which we are bound.

And so to you, as students: One of the surer ways of coming to that recognition is through the fullest understanding possible of this moment. It is a complex consequence of complex past moments. Unless you orient your mind in relation to your past, you will be doomed to the mind's illusion of inwardness. No one will understand you, because you do not understand yourself. To assume that, through a rejection of even a part of your inheritance, you may move outward in a "progress" (to use one of the god-terms that afflict us) is an illusion. To wander in the world that can but appear to us a desert, without any guide separate from the immediate place at which we happen to be at this present moment, is to be lost, however much we may disguise through the spectacle of agitated movement that lostness. Through empty cries of progress, we pretend our journey a line of movement to a desirable end, whose true meaning we need not consider so long as we are caught up in an agitated movement.

And so we have come to a welcomed pause, not an end. The clock, the bell, gives once more a deceptive promise of relief, an illusional calling. Out then, into the daylight of the "real world." I give you, for the moment, your freedom—leaving you to discover the joyful servitude latent in it. My final word, a blessing: Fare ye well—in the older and resonant meaning of that phrase.

II | Nurturing the Mind: The Liberal Arts as Heart with Head

How forcible are right words! but what doth your arguing reprove?
—Job 6:25

I feel somewhat presumptuous, lecturing the general faculty of a liberal arts institution, a faculty whose cumulative labors through several disciplines ought properly to make me cautious. A proper caution, I tell myself, is prelude to one of those virtues most desirable in the academy, indeed which were the central concern of educational institutions. Of course, any explicit address to the traditional virtues, except apologetically as historical footnote, has long since been lost piecemeal to the grinding changes in curricula. Curricula have been redesigned and marketed in the interest of a product—the most advanced student—in some of the ways we redesign and market new automobiles. Curricula are now sets of tools for adjusting the setting of the intellectual machine so that, when a given raw intellect has gone through the process—has been ground and polished—it may be labeled by its speciality and placed on the open market. Such an intellect is modelled by a calibrated curriculum, and is serviceable enough in very restricted operations, though thank God there survives enough resilience in the machine operators—namely us faculty—a sufficient echo of old hungers, to keep most of us from being ourselves simply tools designed by a system whereby other tools for the system may be produced. The catchword justifying such operations is *professionalism,* a term which, as used, carries now little recognition of the professional intellectual calling that was once assumed to order the academy. This is a point I spoke of in talking with your students. It is the point I wish to engage initially here, toward encouraging you in a concern for genuine professionalism. Let us recall something of what the term once meant, in relation to our world's neglected intellectual virtues.

If I say that, fortunately, we are not so distorted in our professionalism but that we remember something of its older and sounder meaning, I do not entirely celebrate that latent memory. For the vague memory itself causes us ample confusions, individually and collectively. Though the memory have root in an old concern for the wholeness of our humanity, it may consequently tempt us to pervert the specialities in which we are trained into a universal authority not truly ours. Vestigial memory of genuine professionalism attaches to intellectual specialization, the specialization itself used as warrant of a general authority—not only *used,* which is bad enough, but *accepted* by community at large as significant warrant. The spectacle of a *limited* authority advanced as general authority is before us constantly in the day's news, which suggests that the academic's abuse is not unique. A movie star, having performed in a popular movie in the role of farm wife, testifies before a congressional committee on the nation's farm problem. A baby doctor, having become a household name to two generations of parents through his program of child rearing, is accepted as expert in international politics.

Examples to the point, as I say, are in this evening's news. What these appearances have in common is the old confusion between spectacle and action, about which Aristotle spoke with great precision in examining classical drama. With the advances in media technology, the present moment of history is the drama we watch, and spectacle is the hook that holds our eye. The evening television news is an abbreviated, episodic melodrama, the episodes selected, reduced, and ordered in such a way that the old distinction between history and art is removed. So successful has the process been that an enlarged version, the "docudrama," promising to be both informative and entertaining, floods the networks. In general these fail both as historical document and as drama, but they manage in doing so to distort our sense of both history and art. And these perversions are often paid for, one notices, by a special media genre, the thirty-second spot ad. These ads appropriate our superstitious obeisance to science in the selling of a headache pill or woman's private toiletries, or they entice us to beer or beef or to a certain new automobile by associating the fad hero of the moment with the product. In either direction, our old commonsense attitudes toward the nature of reality serve us poorly because of our faith in speciality as warrant of general authority. If 85 percent of the doctors polled say they would choose brand X headache tablet if marooned on an island—well, after all, doctors know what is good for us. If the latest star athlete or movie star or popular musician drinks this beer or soft drink—well, it follows as the cattle the belled goat in the stockyard at Chicago that the drink is *the* drink. Not long since, the popular question was what book or piece of music one might wish to be marooned with, not what aspirin tablet, even as it was more largely understood, though not universally, that one was drawn to the hero of a tragedy in a catharsis, not to a thirst-quenching drink of some sort through a superficial association-ism—that is, through a spectacle freed of character in the legitimate sense of the term *character*.

My concern is not with Nielsen ratings or the effectiveness of thirty-second spot ads by that cyclops that so largely holds the family hostage. I am concerned with those failures of commission and omission on the part of the academy that make such spectacle acceptable, that even allow these to be among the most important concerns of family life. The distinction here, as with the distinction between spectacle and action, is crucial. Since they are intellectual distinctions, they are especially crucial to the academy. For the academy is charged with perfections of the intellect in community, so that the central concerns and recognitions might indeed be central to community. In our world, not doctors on an island but all of us are threatened by isolation, by the pressures upon the individual to conclude himself an islanded being almost beyond relief. Modern philosophy has moved toward solipsism, insofar as it takes any position. And when it adopts a sterile relativistic stance, subscribing to no position but only describing positions available, the pretense of a value-free intellectual address to fundamental questions turns out to be but the solipsistic position in disguise, the most pervasive of all hidden agendas. The individual is less person than number in our political or social evaluations, though he may be considered a whole community of contending forces in those psychological evaluations of him. Each segment of himself is shown struggling with every other. Whether deliberately or through instinct, the ad maker is very effective with his island isolation in relation to headache remedy. For he quickly tunes to the authority of those specializations attractive to our vague longing for a reassurance that existence has meaning. He is especially constant in providing the last priest of the last religion in which we have rested general confidence, the Doctors of Science. (Of course, the ad never specifies *medical* doctors, as I recall; no doubt Ph.D.'s holding communications specialities are worthy participants in these aspirin polls.)

What I am suggesting is that the academy is itself very largely the carrier of this disease that both feeds and feeds upon the isolation of the self. It has become so since abandoning its true professionalism, its proper calling as minister to a community of minds among persons, through which mind the body politic might be kept in good, balanced health. That body of course ought to be free to drink Coke or beer if it wish, or even watch docudrama so long as it does not confuse the drinking with social elevation or the docudrama with either history or high art. The academy is properly charged with these intellectual distinctions, whether it receive or accept the charge or not. It is charged with perfections of intellect lest anarchy in the community mind make community itself susceptible to the machinations of the brokers of power, whose goods for sale turn out to be, in the final reckoning, not drink nor other product but the very isolated members of the community themselves. Numbers of islanded souls are accumulated and directed to distorted ends—economic, political, and social.

It is in the academy, then, that the neophytes of mind ought to learn that the presence of a kindly Dr. Spock in a forum on international political issues or a beautiful Sissy Spacek talking about the farm problem before a congressional committee is a matter of spectacle. Such display is planned accident, dramatized by the media in such a way as to be accepted as substance by the audience of such drama. One has, in other words, instant docudrama in the news program—a reflection of neither reality nor of the virtues of art. In such media dramas (and the congressional committee or the forum organizer knows this full well) the specialization of the witness—the actor in the scene—is a costume intended to convince us of sound body beneath. Of course, there is no reason to suppose that Dr. Spock is necessarily wrong in his political ideas, nor Miss Spacek in her ideas about agriculture's complex problems, simply because each is a specialist, the one as a pediatrician, the other as an actress. But we must not conclude that *because* they are established names in these specializations they are therefore credentialled beyond their special names.

I must repeat, lest I be misunderstood: Neither Dr. Spock nor Miss Spacek are to be denied responsible positions on questions other than their specializations. The point is that the spectacles of their particular callings—their public costumes or uniforms as it were—are insufficient certification of their authority. And yet it is the costume that the manipulators of image depend upon to be persuasive to the general public. The spectacle-hungry (if spectacle-jaded as well) are easily confused on the point, and the ease with which they are so confused is, I believe, evidence of the failure of the academy in its responsibilities to community. Confusing spectacle and accident as substance, one contributes to the growing chaos in the community. Oedipus, in respect to his role, has the designation of a special office; he appears to us as King of Thebes. But his tragic mask reminds us that he is not a wise king, a discovery his actions reveal to us and to himself as the play develops, making the tragic mask more significant of the substance of action than is the symbolic crown he wears. The spectacle of his office—crown and kingly robes—is insufficient to the good health of Thebes, so that Oedipus is a tragic hero, not a wise leader of the polis. He himself discovers the considerable difference between a wit sufficient to solve the Sphinx's riddle and a resonant wisdom necessary to one's being father to his people.

I have been charging that the academy is a principal source of intellectual confusions, of such confusions as that between spectacle and action of mind. Even the professors of a liberal arts education are too often the source of this confusion. Let me demonstrate what I mean by local example. In my own institution the faculty of arts and sciences redesigned its bachelor of arts degree and so tailored it in the interests of specialized training (while paying lip service to a liberal education) that now a student, for his humanities requirement, need take only two courses. He may choose them from courses in French literature in translation, German literature in translation, comparative literature in translation, English literature surveys, American literature surveys, classical culture surveys. That is, he is required to take two courses, but he may take them in any order and any combination, from a list of ten to fifteen courses. When he has completed his requirement—say the second half of an American survey course and the second half of an English survey course—he will not have possessed himself of a humanized mind, though his degree will certify that he has partaken of the humanities. I do not cite my own institution as exceptional, obviously. I believe it typical of a general attitude toward liberal arts in the American academy.

The student, either in deference to academic authority as he finds it or in collusion with it, will assume himself inoculated by the humanities virus. He will perhaps be inclined as well, such is human nature in concert with the spirit of our age, to suppose himself certified to hold a valid opinion on such questions as the desirability of Latin and Greek in a liberal arts training. In my first lecture I cited just such an authority, a graduate student in research marketing who rejects as irrelevant any liberal arts training. Such a narrowing, which we are pleased to promote through "PR" as a broadening of the student, exacerbates the problems of the academy. Once our Greek and Roman heritage has been jettisoned, next will be jettisoned most of our Western patrimony, the students very willing participants for the most part, as their gravitation to the second half of English and American literature courses suggests. For if they *must,* for the certificate to employer, have two, these are the closest to them (and to many of their teachers). These are, in a recent catchword, more "relevant" as the necessary consequence of being merely recent history, though why one should really read Wordsworth or Hardy or eighteenth- and nineteenth-century American writers is difficult for them to imagine.

But then I began by saying that I speak to you with some feeling of presumptuousness that ought to prompt caution in me. What I have said hardly seems cautious. It may indeed appear an irresponsibly sweeping indictment, like shouting "Fire!" in this gathering of fire fighters. To insist as I have that academics themselves are largely responsible for such confusions, and none more certainly than faculties of arts and sciences, requires a book to demonstrate. I must be content to appeal to your long memory of your devotions as teachers and trust that thus I may at least open up the possibility that I am right, while I plead my authority on the point: my own thirty-five years devoted to liberal arts education. What I may do, here and now at least, is clarify what I mean by the caution I seem to lack a sufficient measure of. I'd like to do so by suggesting that caution is sometimes prelude to a most desirable virtue, indeed that virtue of all virtues which is most crucial to professionalism, if the term *professionalism* is to signify beyond surface shibboleth—beyond institutional advertising slogan at about the level of selling soap or automobiles. The virtue to which caution is prelude is prudence. And here I take recourse to the authority of an eminent scholastic, a fully professional academic mind, that of St. Thomas Aquinas.

Prudence, says St. Thomas, is the intellectual virtue appropriate to man's reason. Prudence guides and perfects reason so that reason may be suitably disposed to man's proper ends. Prudence is given to the rectitude of the will, so that one has a right reasoning about human act itself, whether that human act be my addressing you now or your teaching a law of physics or a sonnet by Wordsworth tomorrow. Prudence maketh a full intellect, which is to say that prudence allows an ordinate attention to the ends which reason pursues in its attempt to arrive at a perfection of potential being. Through a reason governed by prudence, one neither violates his own good nor the possible good in others. That is why such a guide is most necessary to those who would help others develop the mind each has, without distorting or subverting that mind from its own proper attention to its own good and the good of others.

Through prudence, then, the professor intends to avoid violating the potential integrity of particular minds. But prudence in the conduct of any calling requires that one not avoid the pursuit of desirable ends through timidity, any more than that one should embrace the distorting confusions of intellectual arrogance. A professor professes, or else he should be called something else. Names ought to signify with as close a reference to truth as our naming power allows. Of course, when one professes prudently, he may give the appearance of presumptuousness rather than of the authority of his calling. But that is appearance only. That is, it seems merely spectacle when in truth it must be action ordinately clothed in spectacle insofar as one truly professes. Not that one's students are always aware of the distinction, though most will know the difference through their bones if not their heads, even in bone-head English. For we are marvelously tuned to the vibrations of reality, even when untrained, education being the stringing of a bow suitable to the fiddle each of us is. The end, let me anticipate, is that concert of heart and head which produces whatever music is in us according to our discrete gifts. On this point I shall have more to say presently. Now, however, I must make a peripheral point, seemingly relevant merely to the etiquette of conduct—that surface of manners that is always in flux and so always confusing for us. But manners, we must come to see, are anchored in the integrity of persons as they relate to the integrity of community, without which community must at last be governed merely by letter of the law from which the spirit is absent.

Now one professing presumptuously may appear rather more authoritative than presumptuous to the student himself. That is why students are so easily lead astray by clever minds. They have, at least at some point in their educational histories, an open inclination to accept authority under the very personal necessity of engaging a complex if not frightening world, whether the word of the multiplication tables or, in John Crowe Ransom's tenderly romantic phrasing of it, the names of "all the pretty Kings of France." Our tender concern accompanies each Johnny or Susie, the names that the grammar school principal uses in his mothering of intellect. But just as we do not as educators encourage growth beyond this first infant nurturing of the intellect, neither do we post those signs of expected maturity along the way. What I have to suggest about the desirable guides to this progress of mind from kindergarten to independence, the signs that need posting in relation to our individual gifts of intellect, I must reserve till the next lecture. I wish here only to encourage a distinction between an adult authority and the merely presumptuous in our manner, since manner ought properly to be a sign of authority. Let me reduce these abstractions to particulars. Our students at college level, at least lately, are thought to wish us to use their first names. Sometimes they even request it. Invariably, when I gather information about them on a three-by-five card (name, hometown, prerequisite courses taken) they will give me not only their formal name but a nickname or family familiar name—underlined to indicate that this is what I should call them.

I have a point far more important than what may appear as

only a humorous triviality here. For there is an inappropriate violation of the person of a student whose name is Susan Glockenspiel, whose parents call her "Sissy," if I presume to call her "Sissy." She thinks she would be more comfortable if I did so. At the least, so the tide has run for two decades, I ought to use her first name in calling the roll. But to use a student's first name on the first day of class, I suggest, denigrates our relationship, as if by its use the professor were made an instant familiar. A person's given names and inherited surname have an intricate relationship to a person's being and to his relations in and to the world at large. We are baptized by given name, I tell my students, but then God knows us more intimately than a professor can, does, or even should. Like the earned silence of St. Thomas which I spoke of earlier, one's use of given names is a mutually earned prerogative, demanding more than merely the consent of the student or the presumption of the student's teacher. In some of the Romance languages, there is recognition of the point at issue in the "familiar" mode of pronouns, out of Latin origins. If one is familiar with someone or something, he has through that *familiarity* taken a person or thing into his *family*—a person among friends and family, a piece of knowledge or an idea among the gatherings of his mind. If one is too *familiar,* such has been our recognition of that word's depths, he is presumptuous. To use a student's first name is to force oneself into his "family" prematurely, to assume an intimate relationship yet to be earned. That is from the professor's point of view. From the student's, it will seem thereby to have given the student leave for an unearned admission into that family of mind which it is the professor's responsibility to bring the student to at last. One does not, as we put it, barge in on a family, either the family of mind or of persons. To presume such action is to make of etiquette merely spectacle, rather than language of deportment toward the complex world through manners profoundly taken. We ought to be aware that etiquette shifts so rapidly that new editions of Emily Post are yearly required. But even more, we ought to be aware that this very necessity speaks community decay. First names may be the "in" thing this decade, but with no established relation to the truth of our membership in community.

If then prudence may be formally said to be the application of ethics to practice, manners are the modes of our public acknowledgment and presentation of the complexity of ethics. When we lose sight of this, etiquette becomes comic—becomes matter for satiric ridicule. I doubt that any Southerner is unaware of this conditional attitude toward Southern manners, though I contend it a failure in the perceiver to discover manners as deeper than the spectacle of etiquette. The Southern manner of speech is mimicked in public media—by those we Southerners call Yankees—with such an overplus of intellectual ignorance as to be disturbing, the most signal instance being the treatment of our *you all*. One might point out, of course, Christ's use: "Drink you all of this, which is my blood." Or, turning the satiric tables, though the point would need to be explicated to be effective, Shakespeare's Prince Hal says, in *King Henry IV,* Part I, quietly and aside: "I know you all, and will a while uphold / The unyok'd humour of your idleness." He is speaking of Falstaff, Poins, and that rabble of wit and profligacy. What we observe is that Hal speaks to them in absentia, that he has now risen in a formal manner of address to them and the world, signalled by Shakespeare's shifting the dramatic words out of prose into blank verse. Reflection would tell us that, were the rogues present, Hal would use the same address, "you all," but would speak directly to Falstaff, though including the peripheral others. That, of course, is what happens when we Southerns say "You all come"—caricatured inevitably as "Y'awall come." It is a plural, spoken to a person representing a plurality. You and yours come. It is a familiar, so recognized by those who understand the proper uses of the familiar.

If prudence is the application of ethics to practice, it must follow that such words as *caution* or *deference* or *prudence* have little to do essentially with *timidity* or *shyness* or *self-deprecation,* or any number of words one might choose to suggest self-preservation. The prudent man is at risk in his prudence. The mind which abandons prudence is not thereby heroic, nor is that mind which in the name of prudence refuses risk, for thus he but takes the name of prudence in vain. Such distinctions Shakespeare expects us to be capable of, as he expects us to observe that a Falstaff can use etiquette when he chooses, though divorced of manners in its profound sense. Shakespeare plays Falstaff cleverly against Hotspur within this complex of understanding. Falstaff insists as an aside, lest his cowardice be ridi-

culed: "To the latter end of a fray and the beginning of a feast /
Fits a dull fighter and a keen guest." Not that his aside is not
heard, for the words are in fact spoken in Prince Hal's hearing,
as Falstaff well knows. From his subsequent actions we know
Falstaff subscribes to what he says here, but by mimicking Hal's
high style, with playful wit and prosody, he disengages himself
from the words as bearing his true witness. He bears false witness, a point Shakespeare has made certain we are aware of in
Prince Hal's "You all" speech.

Meanwhile, we have heard Hotspur on the question of bearing witness to his profession of honor, a most stirring speech in
which prudence is conspicuous by its absence. The speech thus
foreshadows the inevitable end Hotspur is bound for:

> By Heaven, methinks it were an easy leap,
> To pluck bright Honour from the pal-fac'd moon,
> Or dive into the bottom of the deep,
> Where fathom-line could never touch the ground,
> And pluck up drowned Honour by the locks;
> So he that hath redeemed her thence might wear
> Without corrival all her dignities.

Honor has quite other meaning for Falstaff. In Act V, we see him
standing over the fallen body of an honorable rebel, Sir Walter
Blunt, and declaring, "There's honour for you! Here's no vanity!" We have just heard him run through his catechism on
honor, this time just out of the hearing of Prince Hal, who has
ordered him into the battle against the rebels. *Honor* for Falstaff
is at best the air used to say the word, a conclusion he comes to
with Scholastic wit in a model instance of intellectual subversion
of prudence:

Can honour set to a leg? No. Or an arm? No. Or take away the grief of a
wound? No. Honor hath no skill in surgery, then? No. What is honour?
A word. What is in this word honour? What is that honour? Air; A trim
reckoning. Who hath it? He that died o' Wednesday. Doth he feel it? No.
Doth he hear it? No. 'Tis insensible, then? Yea, to the dead. But will it
not live with the living? No. Why? Detraction will not suffer it. Therefore
I'll none of it. Honour is a mere scutcheon; and so ends my catechism.

Now, I am pleased that we are still able to be amused by Falstaff's
argument. If it were otherwise, our situation would be desperate
indeed. Or, in honor of Falstaff's wit—no honor to him—I should

perhaps say our spiritual circumstances would be grave indeed. For we are amused precisely because we know this at once to be false catechism. We believe yet that there is much more to honor than either Falstaff's empty breath or Hotspur's confusion of honor with spectacle because he is so much taken with spectacle; it represents for Hotspur notoriety. We see that the dead Blunt and the living Prince Hal between them have notarized honor more significantly. We know that prudence requires neither cowardice nor bravado—that its true exercise is a steady habit of mind in which we pursue proper ends through the limits of our gifts of mind and spirit and body. Contrary to Falstaff's specious argument, honor outlives the honorable man, an evidence of which is our humorous response to Falstaff's catechism.

And so, having said these high things of prudence as the virtue central to professionalism—whether one be destined king of England, rebel soldier, or tavern wit—I recall us to prudence's most central importance to academic professionalism. In all these callings, prudence underlies the integrity of person, but nowhere more crucially than in the academy. I hope to have exorcised that feeling of my own presumptuousness with which I began and even to have put you somewhat at your ease, insofar as you may have feared a lecturing to you on *your* responsibilities as teacher. Those responsibilities surely are yours to discover and honor, not mine to lecture you on, except insofar as I may bear witness to my own discoveries and concerns.

Out of my discoveries, I fear that in the long battles through which the central place of virtue in the academy has been lost, or seemingly lost, the defenders of virtue have weakened the battle lines precisely because they have presumed that virtue may be inculcated—as if a Falstaff might be reformed by Hal's wit or reason or his direct order to reform. No virtue may be planted in another mind as we plant pine seedlings in Georgia or South Carolina barrens with a reasonable expectation of growth toward harvest. Alas, one cannot teach virtue or integrity. One may only bear witness of them, maintaining within oneself that virtue Hope. We may properly hope that some of those to whom we bear witness may be thereby encouraged to recover right-mindedness. St. Thomas, one of my elected fathers of the mind, says that "the purpose of the study of philosophy is not to learn what others have thought, but to learn how the truth of things stands." That, let me suggest, is the good end that any academic mind must pursue with integrity: "to learn how the truth of things stands." In that pursuit, both prudence and hope are much to be cultivated.

What must be remarked in this statement from Thomas is the implicit recognition of my point, namely that truth cannot be transplanted into a mind, any more than virtue can be. What we may teach, and must teach, is what others have thought about the idea of the self or of the nature of the proton or structure of the chromosome or the unity of an ode by Keats. Through such exercise, a mind may learn from what is necessarily a slow and arduous journey under its own power that its end is an encounter with truth and an accommodation of itself to truth, rather than of truth to itself. The labors invite exposition, explication. Under the pressures of time and numbers in the academy of our day, those labors get reduced sadly to fill-in-the-blank and multiple choice accountings of the journey. But neither full exposition nor a successful passing of true-false statements is the proper end— only a means to that end, an encounter with how the truth of things stands.

For us, teaching always risks the dangers of confusing spectacle of mind with action of mind. That is why paper grading is so difficult a task. It is also why so many teachers appear to their students as "characters" with amusing eccentricities, sometimes (let us confess) an appearance cultivated by us teachers. But the confusing of spectacle with action is a danger already implicit in the very mode required of teaching, the use of words. How tempting, seeing an immediate effect of one's words upon an audience, to shift the moment's concern to effect, to play before an audience. Analysis demonstrated by analogy makes poets of us all, and happily so—so long as analogy does not become an end itself whereby the *unlikeness* in like things is all but lost. It is an arresting reflection, for instance, that insofar as our instruments of the moment—including our minds—can measure such a position, man exists midway between the extremities of outer space and particle physics. To stand midway between the proton and the outer galaxies by an act of the imagination is fascinating reflection, worth engaging in relation, say, to the medieval world picture in which man also occupies the crucial middle in the syllogisms of being.

But how tempting, given not only the seductions of our own minds but the external pressures in the academy, to make a spectacle of truth. I have noticed one of our own academic vice-presidents praising an honors professor in public ceremony, saying of this political science teacher that he "goes to considerable effort to dramatize his teaching." If he is the character in his course, the protagonist at the center of his science of politics, little honor to him. On the other hand, the poet of the *Song of Roland* yields to a similar temptation to captivate audience and continue its captivity. Seeing an excitement in his audience over the slaughter of a common enemy, the poet hauls in another hundred thousand Saracens to delay Turpin's and Oliver's and Count Roland's inevitable end. Thus spectacle as substance may be praised by poets or teachers, though the danger always is that they themselves may displace the central focus of truth. So, too, may a visiting lecturer.

Our general concern continues to be prudence—prudence to the academician. And more locally, we are speaking of spectacle in relation to action as governed by prudence. It would be no escape of the temptation to spectacle, let us say, if one resort merely to busywork as an exorcism of personality in one's professionalism. An accumulation of facts and statistics, severely ordered, may seem an escape from showmanship, but the risk is that facts and numbers may steal the show, bear false witness to truth. "All the *pretty* kings of France" is larger and fuller insight toward truth than "all the kings of France." It is a risky profession, ours—the more so since there no longer exists a general intellectual climate within which one knows by the breathing of it that an integrity of mind is a habit to be acquired and not transmitted. One needs reminding that his integrity is one he comes to. We do not possess it by reason of birth or of formal preliminary training. Insofar as we individually acquire that habit, I believe we are less susceptible to the temptation to distort our words. We discover a professional deportment toward truth which requires that we bear witness to the virtues of intellect. Not an easy nor comfortable task, but we may remember a synonym of *witness* is *martyr.*

It is a discovery we must embrace and maintain against the odds in these grim times. How does one make it clear to a world given to pragmatic ends that such integrity is the true measure of any professor of mind, any witness or martyr to the truth that mind is man's peculiar gift? One is represented to the general world by such superior authority as the academic affairs officer who testifies under oath that she prefers (and I quote) "to err on the side of making a mistake" when passing athletes who have not passed. Or again, how, in a climate of pragmatic goals, may one make known that only the alchemist of the sixteenth and seventeenth centuries would be so bold as to assert emphatically, as a president of a major university has done in championing biotechnology, that "we must find a way to reprogram nature"? Under the burden of having one's professional position defined by one's specialization as judged by such minds as those, the measure itself will inevitably become the number of pages published and the supposed reputation of the journals in which one's words appear. One will be weighed by the number of hours devoted to a number of courses that hold a number of students. We shall then accept as valid the number of credits certified for a student and thereby signify the student himself, now full of credit hours, a specialist. Spectacle thus overwhelms significant action in the academy, from the top to the bottom, leaving the individual professor feeling at times at an isolated midpoint, from which his administration is as far removed as an outer galaxy, his student as far removed as the proton.

It has not been easy for me, nor for you I am certain, to make clear to others in our larger community that my profession is a calling; that I am a professor on 24-hour call, 365 days a year. I am reminded of the odds against professional integrity every time I receive a notice to be filled out certifying the number of articles or books or papers given in an academic year; the number of sick leave days I claim; the number of holidays taken; the number of committees I've served on, or theses directed. Academic spectacle, signified by such routines, is a present confusion always, making it most difficult to maintain the principles of a professionalism without which the academy becomes only some species of trade school—which schools, incidentally, I highly approve of, so long as they do not advertise themselves as universities.

To summarize my alarm by example once more, I have from my chief academic officer, the one already cited, a notice given with the authority of law: The academic deans are reminded that each instructor is "to adhere to the 2500-minute requirement" for the 5-hour course. Classes are to meet "the required number of contact minutes," whether engaged in sixth-grade grammar for college credit or wrestling with the ideas of Plato and Aristotle. In collusion with such an administrative approach to professionalism, the student is required to evaluate the teacher on the basis of the 2,500 contact minutes. That testimony becomes reduced to statistics, affecting the daily bread which even professors in chairs cannot forego, given how fallen professors are since the days of Origen. I say "since Origen," remembering the student evaluation given him, his assistants calling him *chalkenteros*—that is, "a worker with brazen bowels." Brass-bowelled Origen received epic epithet as his student evaluation. Socrates received a capital one in 399 B.C. Our evaluations tend to be somewhat less arresting, though not without their moments, too. A student wrote of a colleague of mine that "Professor X did such a good job that by the end of the quarter he was useless." As with our amusement over Falstaff's catechism, these words delight by their inadequacy to the truth to which they would bear witness. But for good or ill, the remark will be tabulated and used for or against my colleague to graph his academic integrity through abstract numbers. And one who prefers to err on the side of making a mistake can use such graphs for or against one.

Aside from the inherent dangers of our calling, the circumstances are not themselves propitious. But given all the obstacles to our prudential witness of our profession, our habit of intellectual integrity, we are not willing to abandon our calling, though many in the lower public schools, and among them the best, are increasingly doing so. Of that calling I have yet more to say. I would bear my own witness to certain principles we either hold in common or might in my view properly hold. In my opening lecture to your students I touched upon a sound cliché which I repeat to you: To use the wrong word is to bear false witness. I shall certainly not intend to use the wrong word as I attempt to use words to celebrate our common calling, though if I do so, yours is the responsibility to help clarify and make the word more precise. I have with you, as with your students, every confidence that you will sort out what I have next to say—that you can and will discount spectacle, except insofar as it is soundly anchored in a prudent action of my mind. My happiest end would be that you might, by the end of this series, discover that I, to you, like my colleague to his student, am completely useless as you turn afresh to your professional callings.

What is this common calling we share? At the risk of sounding like a Falstaffian catechism, let me suggest the following. Professors—that is, those who profess through words to bear witness to truths encountered so that others may by their own actions move toward truth—professors are first and foremost stewards of a common property, for which by the nature of their office they must bear a common concern. This is the principle that makes of a faculty of arts and sciences, when properly constituted, a community of scholars as opposed to an abstract structure of divisions, departments, schools, or colleges. Without such community of responsibility, given the divisiveness of specialization, a faculty must be at last inadequate to its community calling, to its being a body devoted to mind. The effect upon the community of mankind is anything but humorous, though one might construct a Swiftian parable to suggest just how unacceptable such abstract structures may be. I have in mind only the seed of such a parable, sufficient to our purposes. Imagine a school of veterinary medicine, broken into factions in consequence of specializations which are directed toward its clients in the animal world. There are the avians on the one hand and on the other the large and small animal specialists, a division itself susceptible to civil war. Or in biology, there are the microbiologists on the one hand and on the other the whole-organ behaviorists, each division capable of inordinate devotion to its speciality. An Aldous Huxley or George Orwell might make a marvelous fictional parable of either, the point of which would be the unfortunate effect upon chickens, dogs, horses, humans with liver conditions or the like malady.

The common property which a community of scholars holds in fee simple, we said, is words, in all of the manifestations of words. That is why it is destructive of academic community when the chemistry teacher relegates the crying problem of subject-verb agreement in his student's brief answers to the English department, or when the English professor abandons the implications of history in the poetry of Shelley, or when the history professor ignores the philosophical and theological problems attendant upon the publication of the *Origin of Species*. But one professing a calling within the community of scholars may by a narrowed vision of his calling contribute to our abandoning common responsibility. That is, there is a safety afforded the professional by his specialization. I remark here a considerable contribution made by departments of English to Johnny's inability to read or write. In large part the direct cause is the English department's eager assumption of a general responsibility for reading and writing. Departments were quick to seize such restricted authority, since the technical face of words as used by students seemed so promising as pragmatism came to dominate universities. Such power allowed prestige to English departments, who otherwise found it increasingly difficult to justify their existence. Science became ascendant in the public's regard, and so by borrowed analogy grammar, punctuation, elementary composition put on the robes of science. An elementary "science" of words borrowed authority from the prestigious "hard" sciences of matter through empirical logic, and each found itself increasingly sealed off from the other, eventually making "Arts *or* Sciences" a more appropriate title for colleges within universities. The end result has been—dare we say it?—that university courses in sixth-grade grammar are now the principal justification for the existence of departments of English across the country, that "service" role used by them to support their own dying major and graduate degree programs, through "teaching assistants." Elementary grammar is needed, of course, to prepare students for elementary courses in physics.

I trust I am not so simplistic as to suggest that the professors of history are likely to be learned in questions of ontology and teleology, or to know with full authority the thesis position of a prudent science that would, in Plato's and Aristotle's sense of the phrase, "save the appearances." We are, most of us, after all ourselves products of the education system I have been castigating. I am bold enough to assert, however, that we *ought* to be so learned or ought to be *conscience bound* to attempt to become so learned. Nor am I so far removed from the realities of departments of English as to suppose that teachers of Shelley are well grounded in the developments of Western philosophy since Descartes, though, again, they ought to be, even as they ought to be able to distinguish Wordsworth's thought from Plato's in respect to problems of epistemology and the relations of mind to natural phenomena. Otherwise, they shall not be capable of teaching their students to read Shelley's "Hymn to Intellectual Beauty" or Wordsworth's "Lines Composed a Few Miles Above Tintern Abbey" at a level beyond the ninth or tenth grade.

Between the reality of academic mind as it is at our moment and the desirable realities of the academic mind, there is a great chasm. What I insist as proper to academic integrity is that the academic himself be at least always and acutely aware of the chasm. For only through such awareness will it ever be possible to reach outward from the closed world of one's specialization toward bridging—toward healing—the great wound in the body of the academic mind, the chasm between intellectual *is* and *ought*. The alternative is a continuing and accelerating crumbling along the edges of the chasm, the border of one's speciality, however bright and cheerful a music we make as we struggle against chaos, lured especially by that current pan-music "Back to the Basics." Our music becomes louder and louder as we shout against each other the virtues of the specialized mind, but the anxiously listening world of the larger community hears no symphony. It hears instead a music very like that accompanying the collapse at the Tower of Babel.

To recognize a common failure in the divided academic mind is to begin a recovery, toward becoming a community of scholars, through academic prudence. It is to begin a recovery of professionalism in the high sense I would give the term. Such a recognition will reveal at once, for instance, the imprudent absurdity of a recent statement by a celebrated Oxford professor. Professor Rom Harre of Linacre College says, in his *Philosophy of Science: An Introductory Survey* (Oxford University Press, 1986) under the topic "Metaphysics": "No one of any discretion writes about the Universe, Man, and God." No one of discretion or prudence can make such a statement as Professor Harre's if he has been bold enough to look beyond his crumbling academic province. If one reads Professor Stanley Jaki's Gifford Lectures, given at the University of Edinburgh and published as *The Road of Science and the Ways of God* (1977) by Professor Harre's own press, or Professor Jaki's Freemantle Lectures given at Balliol College and issued by the same press as *The Origin of Science and the Science of Its Origin* (1978)—if one read these prudently meticulous lectures, he cannot avoid talking and writing about the Universe, Man, and God. One who has read Eric Voegelin's great work *Order and History,* or who has followed the fascinating developments in particle physics, cannot avoid, and still maintain intellectual integrity, a concern for those old high topics.

Nor may one—these engaging monuments of unaging intellect aside—look into the recent maverick book by David Berlinski, *Black Mischief: The Mechanics of Modern Science* (William Morrow and Company, Inc., 1986), and miss the point that a Professor Harre confuses spectacle with action. I am not picking on Professor Harre; I am intending only to cite him as an example of a common failure of academic integrity whereby we confuse the truth of complex reality with the limited truth we may have found through our own specialization. The claims Harre makes in the name of science are unsupportable. It may be that he speaks facetiously, though I think not. Berlinski, on the other hand, speaks with scathing irony about the inadequacies of a range of sciences from physics to linguistics, suggesting that we have succeeded only in replacing one primitivism with another. We have, he says, so managed the simplifications of reality that "mechanism comes to replace animism, a historical development in which the mathematical physicist or the molecular biologist takes inordinate and boastful pride."

Black Mischief is, as it were, an inside job. Berlinski is by initial training an "analytic philosopher," with considerable additional training in mathematics, both of which he has taught. He has worked widely in several sciences as well, as an intellectual pilgrim, and so he speaks of biology or physics or behavioral psychology or linguistics from a position informed by considerable labors on the disciplines he questions. The mischief in the book is partly Berlinski's; his position toward science in its currently established authority is that of a knowledgeable iconoclast. But the greater part of the mischief is science's own, black in that its mischief hides a present light in reality by a darkness it declares to be light. It enjoys a devoted laity, this latest of man's religions, among whom there is considerable confusion between the meaning of light and darkness. Berlinski calls attention, for instance, to the elements of personality and prejudice unexamined, the heart's acceptance of the Mosaic laws of science where the head's consent is called for. In our terms, what we see ruling is spectacle paraded as pure action of mind—as if in response to the full truth of things. Berlinski finds pervasive of this scientific mind something which I would describe as a fundamentalist religion, anchored in eighteenth- and nineteenth-century mechanistic philosophy. It is a condition of intellectual fundamentalism that is no longer tolerable to the integrity of the scientific mind properly oriented to its principles and limits, being neither true science nor a science of the true. To quote Berlinski directly: "If mechanism [out of the Newtonian vision of the world] is no longer a reasonable philosophy for the whole of nature, it is a doctrine that retains its fragrant appeal elsewhere—in stock market forecasting, astrology, linguistics, artificial intelligence, future forecasting and catastrophe theory, meteorology, molecular biology and the neo-Darwinian theory of evolution." What engages Berlinski's iconoclastic humor, in this alternately delightfully and irritatingly irreverent book, is the disregarded human element in scientific thought. What one may conclude from his arguments and evidence is that the imperfections out of fundamental human nature even affect so pure an intellectual calling as higher mathematics, let alone the lesser stepchildren of mathematics, the several sciences. And what is amusing to Berlinski is very disturbing to some of us and ought to be to more of us: accepted scientists lacking sufficient recognition of the human presence in science and so of a potential flaw in their vision of reality. With what must seem to many of Berlinski's colleagues impiety spoken by an apostate, Berlinski calls in sharp question the religious fundamentalism of both popular and institutional science. He is no doubt as welcomed by some of his colleagues as Alcibiades at Socrates' banquet, and might indeed be forewarned, given the final student evaluation of Socrates in 399 B.C.

I might have chosen the more orthodox philosophers to make this point about the weakness in science displayed often as dogmatic fundamentalism. Eric Voegelin or Jaki. Or Étienne Gilson in his *From Aristotle to Darwin and Back Again* or his *Linguistics and Philosophy*. But I choose Berlinski's *Black Mischief* since it makes my point without directly engaging the metaphysical position I believe we must at last come to in talking about the Universe, Man, and God. At a reduced level of the encounter of mind with nature—that is, a level short of the metaphysical—Berlinski discovers and describes a radical disparity between the words of science and the realities with which those words purport to deal. His, too, is a concern for the precise use of words, from the perspective of the analytic philosopher, a position requiring him to maintain no commitment for or against science or metaphysics. As he says of his exploration of the catastrophe theory and its critics, "My interest . . . is purely *pour le sport,*" a remark that describes his general interest in the foibles of modern scientists. So, he speaks as a relatively disinterested authority on the intellectual status of modern science, his words an occasion for the sport of analysis itself.* His primary concern is for the word used precisely within the laws of logic. Hence he confines his concern to the relation of mind to the world as revealed in words, but leaves suspended the relation of mind to the world of nature and to the supernatural—the metaphysical realm.

In our pursuit of the truths of existence through science, says Berlinski, "the sheer volume of current scientific work is often taken as evidence for the vibrancy of scientific culture." Sheer volume gives an illusion of vibrancy to our academic culture. And his point about science bears extension beyond the limits of science alone, sheer volume of publication in other disciplines being notorious, as anyone struggling to be promoted in academic rank

---

* In one department Berlinski is less than disinterested: linguistics, in which he is obviously fascinated. In particular he is warmly drawn to Noam Chomsky's ideas, sometimes I think at the expense of reality. His analysis of the two planes of language—letters and words—and the statistical evaluation of the interplay between those planes is so enticing that he provides no presence of mind in the planes; they appear existences independent of man, like nature's butterflies. This oversight is out of his special fascination for generative language. Otherwise, he has the arrogant flair of Joyce's Stephen Dedalus, an intellectually refined wit that is particularly devastating on reductionisms. A reader might feel at times an absence of resonance in Berlinski for all his mastery of words, which is why Voegelin, Jaki, or Gilson are finally more dependable. One's discomfort is a bit like that of being forced into the company of a very precocious child. But there is relief from the alternate delight and irritation of the experience: One reads more or less independent sections, rather than a sustained treatise; Berlinski's structure is dictated by an imaginative, creative bent in words and through them, again as with Joyce's Stephen. As with Joyce's *Portrait,* one can lay *Black Mischief* aside and return to it if one wishes to. Meanwhile, it is well to turn to Gilson's tribute to Chomsky as linguist, in *Linguistics and Philosophy.* Gilson rather carefully establishes an ordinately just judgment of both linguistics as a science and Chomsky's contribution to it because Gilson's judgment is out of a thorough exploration of thought as distinct from words, an exploration glowing with wonder but not distorted by enthusiasm.

knows well. $E=MC^2$ can be written on a three-by-five card, but try to convince the usual promotion committee of its profundity when weighed against thirteen articles and the beginning of a book on the cultural impact of rock 'n' roll music on the aspirations of youth, or a long study detailing the quality of life in society as measured by the number of refrigerators and indoor toilets in limited geographical areas. Or try to persuade the president of a university that, in Berlinski's words, "what physics has to offer the rest of us is a matter of style, not content." Or that a principal virtue of the theory of perfect competition in a school of economics is "the ease with which it can be taught to undergraduates." How disturbing to academic order if we must conclude, as our author does, that "every science rests on concepts that it accepts but cannot rigorously explain" or that "science has historically been most successful when it ignores the grossness of complexity and treats instead a sparse and elegant universe in which point masses, for example, replace planets and numbers come to stand for properties." The statements need only a substitution of *religion* for *science* and brief commentary to reveal these the old judgments upon the relevance of religion to reality made by eighteenth-century rationalism.

Again, please do not misunderstand what I am saying in my own person. I do not argue that such simplifications of reality are necessarily improper to valid science. When one is concerned with a virus—its properties and remedy—the virus becomes the world for the mind's attention. But something would be radically wrong if, through such a study, the scientist in his specialized concern for the virus could no longer see anything but viruses wherever he turned. He might, were he dealing with the AIDS virus, become sufficiently terrified that he might withdraw from all creation, fearing that there is no defense against Being—Existence—in general, all Being now mistaken for viruses. When we lose sight of the fact that in specializations of any sort we engage in simplifications of the mystery of existence, we are likely to promote dogma to absolutist doctrine whereby we may either flee existence or rise superior to it, either movement destructive of our own complex being as persons in nature at a particular juncture of history. To be naïve about synecdoche is to fail as poet: To express the whole through the name of a part is an acceptable rhetorical device, but to mistake the part as the whole is prelude to intellectual disaster, since the whole will always reassert itself against such reductionism.

I myself believe, on principles like those of science (that is, on principles that cannot be rigorously explained at the empirical level), that each of us is severally gifted, in consequence of which we are each dependent; we are necessarily members one of another in whatever community we inhabit, whether a small hometown or an academic faculty at a signal, famous institution. I believe as well that we are obligated to perfect our particular gifts; through such perfections we become what we are potentially, in every instance less than God but more than stone or possum. That is why for the good of us all, individually and as communities, we academics are particularly responsible for that common gift whereby we discover distinction and proportion in nature without thereby abandoning kinship to created things. I mean by this common property, once more, language. It follows that, in a community of scholars, there must be established and maintained an integrity of mind whereby the scientist and poet support a common good through the uses of that common property. It is an integrity that begins with the concerted support of orderly discourse. Neither the chemist nor historian should leave grammar or punctuation to the English teacher. The specialization of precision of sense through words cannot be delegated, because it is not special. It is self-evidently common.

I said scientist and poet share this concern in academic community, and lest I be understood as suggesting that only the chemist and the lyricist constitute that community, a clarification. The rational faculty we share, focused on analysis, defines the virus; the rational faculty governing the imagination puts that virus in the context of the whole existence. The offices of analysis and imagination are not themselves mutually exclusive. I know of no great scientist who has not been poet, nor great poet who has not shared with the scientist certain powers of analysis. Our liberal learning is divided between science and art, an artificial division exacerbated for reasons multitudinous, some of which I have spoken of already. But when we urge upon our students the desirability of studying science and art, of being liberal arts majors, we still acknowledge not a separation but complementary roles, even though we do not fully realize the burden of our recommendation. We know, when we are at our best, that in the academic community the elegant simplifications of science are complemented by the intricate enlargements toward ambiguity that philosophy opens. The result for the student, ideally, is a discovery of an abiding intellectual openness to the wonders of existence; wonder and awe are in his seeing, wherever and whenever he turns his mind upon existence. This is but another way of saying that the academic mind, the community we call collectively *faculty,* is both in its collective and individual membership always student to the mystery of existence. What the likenesses are in our seemingly unlike callings of the mind to academic concerns, I should like next to address, though I may be discovered to do so more in the manner of the poet than of either scientist or philosopher. Should I succeed, perhaps you may be persuaded to grant the poet asylum in the academic community, as the scientist has been given such refuge. Here I speak rather more directly of the poet than of historian or philosopher, whose analytic faculties serve the imagination also, and in whom there is necessarily much of the poet. I do not mean, therefore, to subordinate historian or philosopher.

For most of the history of the academic mind, say from the time of Plato's *Republic* to the mid-twentieth century, the poet has been an unwelcomed presence in the formal communities of intellect, welcomed at court at times but not in cloister. That treatment has sometimes led him to whine about his ostracism or to shout against the unjust discrimination, to which it must be admitted he has sometimes contributed just cause. The engagement of the poet with the power established resident on intellectual reservations such as the academy comes to the level of spectacle in the nineteenth century. Shelley insists that the poet be recognized as the "unacknowledged legislator" of the polis, no less influential (such is the implication) than an Edmund Burke. Setting aside Shakespeare, as Ben Jonson was inclined to do since Shakespeare had little Latin and less Greek, and setting aside Chaucer, who was more public man than poet in his own day, it seems reasonable to say that while most English and American poets have been university men, universities have not taken them into the compound as it were. There is a current aberration. Since the 1960s, the anti-academic poets are a required presence in the academy, more nearly because they are anti-academic than because they are poets—as if their presence might help still those disaffected youth who have been so troublesome to the academy. But even these latter-day language Luddites have themselves been, almost to a man, products of the academy, Allen Ginsberg a representative instance. It is as if the academy has asked itself whether anarchy is not the order of art. Concluding it so, and accepting the tradition of art as a requirement in the academy, it has embraced anarchist poets as a necessary presence. But this is a present aberration whose continuance is in doubt. Meanwhile, Milton, Wordsworth, Tennyson—even Shelley—were university men, valued by their institutions. They were valued early, perhaps, rather for their having come and gone than for having settled in the groves about the temples of intellect. The poet was made welcome by the academy—if he was passing through, or if he but camp at a sufficient remove on the outskirts—and, as I have suggested, was often so treated for good reason.

There is an explanation, if not good reason, for such an attitude in the academy, residually received from Plato's arguments. Those Platonic arguments have been narrowly taken by scholars of Plato and verified out of passing experience, as with the evidence of the wild young Shelley at University College, Oxford. The poet is, let us admit, something of a fool. But here I mean *fool* in a higher sense than the term's popular use as epithet. In the medieval world, for instance, the fool was a disquieting presence in the social order for reasons other than that he disturbed the peace in taverns or chapel. Before we smile condescendingly toward the medieval attitude, let us examine it further, so that we may see why I and that old world now largely lost to us speak of the fool as special, as extraordinary, and in many respects as necessary to the fullness of community, even perhaps to the academic one. We may thereby find reason for charity toward colleagues who seem best described by that epithet *fool*, though I am speaking, initially at least, of the congenital fool.

The medieval world understood the fool to be a special instance of humanity, and it did so with less superstition than we suppose of that world—with less sentimentality than is our wont. We to the contrary rest our superstitions in the mystery of genes; knowing genetics (such is our faith), we shall eventually be able to give a full account of beings in the world, especially those left incomplete by nature. The fool, it was thought by our ancient fathers, is somehow out of the order of nature, not merely an aberration of nature. Looking at what we define as the "clinically retarded," we are rather likely to consider such an unfortunate creature only a mistake of nature. A considerable body of opinion, growing out of mechanistic science such as Berlinski exposes in *Black Mischief*, uses such creatures to justify one form or another of euthanasia. Such are the inevitable responses to that sense of power given us under such rubrics as a current one I quote once more: "We must find a way to reprogram nature."

The medieval attitude toward the fool, being more pious toward creation in general than is ours, suspends radical judgment of aberration. It at least suspects the possibility that the fool is somehow a special gift. If the Greek mind considered the stranger at the door very possibly a god or goddess and extended charity to ward off retribution, the medieval mind thought such a stranger certainly one of God's creatures in the likeness of Christ and therefore requiring Christian greeting and welcome. (I am aware of medieval violence, of course, remarking only that one at least was likely to know his enemy in those violent days. It is our world in which friend and enemy are most difficult to distinguish, to the panic of city dwellers in particular. Another of the names of our time, concomitant of the Age of Alienation, is the Age of the Dead-Bolt Lock.) For the medieval mind, the fool might well be a special agent of grace, his apparent mental deformity even possibly a gift of a superior visionary power.

It is quite revealing to contrast the medieval agent, the fool, in family and community with our own attempts to come to terms with a special presence, the child, and see how we respond to such special creation. So much attention has been spent on the child in family and society in the past decade that a considerable library is necessary to keep up with the discussion. I borrow from only the most recent, Professor Stanley Hauerwas's *Suffering Presence* (1986). In considering the current activist cause, "children's rights," Professor Hauerwas remarks the cause is an attempt "to make up for the breakdown of our shared beliefs about how parents should care for their children." Rather than being simply a concern for the rescue of children from brutal abuse, a symptom of the breakdown, it has every appearance of a political movement out of the elevation of the child to the level of citizen. It proceeds from the position that the relation of citizen to citizen is a relation of power, necessarily mediated by governmental superpower. Among the signs of our gradual displacement of the child as child, leading to the current crisis, is the studied casting of the child in adult roles. At home, Mama may well dress Susan as a woman; Daddy has early expectations of Johnny as his "little man." Not new inclinations. But when the schools themselves engage in mock United Nations Assemblies or engage current issues in an activist way through class projects, the child, robbed of childhood, becomes presumptuous adult. The tenor of the times is pitched that way. As Richard John Neuhaus puts the point, "At the deepest level, the 'breakdown' of the family is evident in a parental loss of nerve when parents accept the proposition that their highest goal is to help the child become autonomous." When the structure of a society establishes a relation of citizens to each other as strangers to each other, rather than as members of community, the effect on families within that society begins to reflect the individualistic principles that make each autonomous. Children's rights, such is the next step, will be established by law. The strength of moral understanding which must order society will be replaced by governmental code. We shall then have no place for either the fool or child save in a controlled environment established by the state.

You will remember with what remarkable persuasiveness that unacademic poet Shakespeare raises the possibility of the fool as visionary in his character called simply the Fool, that familiar spirit to King Lear who counterpoints Lear's high sentences with his foolish words that penetrate to depths Lear hasn't recognized in his own increasingly futile words. And I hope you may know, or come to know, another remarkable handling of this mystery of nature, the fool, in a contemporary work. Flannery O'Connor, in her novel *The Violent Bear It Away*, has as catalyst for grace an idiot child named Bishop, whose guardian Rayber considers the child a mistake of nature. As steward of nature under the aegis of science, Rayber feels a moral obligation to obliterate the child. Lest we dismiss the argument as being merely a fiction, we find Peter B. Medawar, the distinguished Nobel biologist, making the same argument in his *Hope of Progress: A Scientist Looks at Problems in Philosophy, Literature and Science.* That Rayber cannot kill the child Bishop he can understand only as a sign of an incipient insanity in himself, inherited biologically. For love itself is an aberration to Rayber. Medawar is not so extreme: For him, it is a matter of education needed to get us over our rather primitive attitudes toward such mistakes of nature; we are ignorant in those matters, not insane.

Having said these things of the fool, we may better appreciate the resonant drama in that old medieval romance *Tristan and Iseult* and recognize through it an abiding truth about the poet as complement to the man of science, though we haven't the time necessary to broaden and level and fill in potholes on that long road from *Tristan and Iseult* to a modern novelist like Miss O'Connor. I recall the passage where Tristan, disguised as a fool after his exile from King Mark's court and from his beloved Queen Iseult, returns to Cornwall. He is welcomed by the porter: "Come in, lord fool." And a cry of welcome goes up from the townsmen: "The fool! the fool!" A crowd gathers, a rout of citizens laughing and shouting and throwing stones at him, escorting him to King Mark. Laughing, Mark greets him, and at the fool's request makes a gift of the queen to the fool in the merriment of the moment. He asks, "If I gave you the Queen, where would you take her, pray?" To which Tristan in the role of fool replies, in one of the great poignant passages of our literature: "Oh, very high . . . between the clouds and heaven, into a fair chamber glazed. The beams of the sun shine through it, yet the winds do not trouble it at all. There would I bear the Queen into that crystal chamber of mine all compact of roses and the morning." Such a lovely residence for a love removed from the shadows of the world has seldom been seen since Socrates' magic words in the *Phaedrus*. To the uninitiated, of course, the words seem wildly removed from all reality, as they do to King Mark and his barons, who laugh and say, "Here is a good fool at no loss for words." To the initiated, to the hearer of the poem, as to Tristan and to Queen Iseult, there is the poignancy of lost love, a trembling hope of recovery so intense as to be almost unbearable. It touches the rose at its canker and briar, the deep wound in our human nature that speaks nature fallen.

I have borrowed from this excruciating love story, full of the mystery of potions as explanation for the canker of inordinate love, in the interest of the poet's true return to the academy from his exile. Remember, though, that poets, like fools, move by indirections in their words, sometimes moving with excruciating slowness—as if not subject to time as are ordinary mortals. But sometimes they do so because they recognize the complexity in the truth of things which never submits to the simplifications of the rationalist's reduction of existence, the "sparse and elegant universe" a scientist may wish to establish. The ways of love are most various. If prudence is the mannerly conduct of intellect in the presence of existence, it is a conduct appropriate to the wooer. Love consumes prudence in the end, but one trusts that the consuming love will be beyond the level of spectacle such as clothes it in *Tristan and Iseult* in the rags of the fool—lest the poet prove only gossip and his words suited to gossip columns and not to the colloquy of the academic community. I move slowly, and by indirection, but I beg your patience yet awhile.

For I have really in mind an argument for the poet as a most necessary presence to the health of academic community. Here I do not intend by the title *poet* such presences as we have remarked popular in the academy since World War II. That community is not likely to be strengthened by a Dylan Thomas or Allen Ginsberg. But it is not the poet as a particular named person I have in mind—a Thomas or Ginsberg. It is the poet resident in each academic mind, however much suppressed therein. That poet needs bringing into an ordinate residence. To rediscover him requires our finding him in the nature of mind itself, in the faculties that constitute mind. The exploration of those faculties is most tempting to one given to seeing likeness in unlike things: The individual mind one might explore as microcosm of the macrocosm we have been calling the academic community, and I believe there is sufficient reason for such a figure—for such a metaphor—based on thoughtful minds as ancient as Heraclitus and on scientific minds as recent as those doing the latest research on our organ the brain in its relation to the mystery of thought. I shall dwell on thoughtful ancient minds here, but encourage you to watch for the latest researches of science into the brain to test my argument—or rather to test my metaphor. We return first to that medieval world out of which Tristan comes laughing and skipping toward us in his agony and so comes into the fragmentation of mind that, in its worldly manifestations, we applaud as the Renaissance. For that escape from what we sometimes characterize as the Dark Ages increasingly appears not an escape *from* but an entrapment *in* a darker age than that old one.

On the poet's behalf, let me suggest that he is not so far removed from the philosopher such as Plato or Aristotle or the scientist such as Bacon or Newton as the caricature of the poet since the Renaissance suggests. That cartoon version of him may be laid largely to a selective use of Plato that begins in the Renaissance, a version which helps account for the relief to the academic mind that our first great academic, Plato, found the poet wanting. So much wanting that, as we all remember, Plato denied the poet citizenship in his republic. And so effective has been this limited version of Plato that we have been able for centuries to blink a most radical pronouncement made by the father of the academy in the *Phaedrus*. It is perfectly true that Plato finds the mimetic poet less than acceptable, that in fact he finds such a poet dangerous, insofar as mimesis is of that shadow of reality we have come to speak of as Nature. And Plato might find that poet's descendant in our day much given to spectacle. One might find him entertaining coffeehouse crowds, for instance, standing on a table to disrobe to the rhythm of his own stream-of-consciousness intellectual masturbation, as if thereby he imitated nature in its most secret alcoves and hidden corners. That has been one of the modern attempts at holding a mirror down to nature, as it were. Freudian and Neo-Freudian academic interests have so certified this poet as intellectual subject that the academy has felt it necessary to find him a place—if not on a table then in a Chair.

It is Eric Voegelin who reminds us of another Platonic poet. In that late work the *Phaedrus*, Plato presents a hierarchy of souls in the community of mankind, setting them in a list of the higher and lower. I do not think Plato would object to my suggesting that this spectrum of souls might be taken metaphorically as inclinations of a single soul—as a microcosm—though I do not intend following each inclination in its geography within each of us. Let us note instead that, though the poet as mimetic artist, his words busy mirrors in pursuit of nature, is ranked sixth from the crowning eminence of all souls in the *Phaedrus*, there is present in the ranking another poet. He is the *philokalos*, the lover of Beauty. He is placed at the very top in equal rank with the *philosophos*, the lover of Wisdom. The poet as lover of Beauty is to the mimetic poet, one might say, as the lover of Wisdom is to the technologist, in which relations I intend no denigration, only that we see in proportion to the realities of existence. The *philokalos* is, as Voegelin remarks, the new poet, the soul possessed by the *mania*. By *mania*, Plato does not mean *madness*, though that is a popular rendering of the idea, sometimes appropriated by the poet himself, sometimes supplied by those suspicious of him. Plato rather means here to describe that impulse in the soul that bursts beyond itself in seeing into the life of things, the visionary poet, of whom Dante is such a welcomed example to the point. This poet's manner, his mode of address to existence, differs from that of the *philosophos*, who seeks insight into the life of things with the aid of the rational faculty.

Little wonder that, as empiricism rises on the one hand and Cartesian gnosticism rises on the other, the poet's role to the public mind appears a clear and present danger. He is a danger, even if he is the *philokalos* rather than the mimetic poet. It is perhaps of more relief to both poets, if the truth were known, that very good poets appear on both sides of that spectacle of factionalism, the beginnings of political specializations, the English Civil War. That political war and even its poetry are rather spectacles of the fragmentation of community than anything else. The politics of Roundhead against Cavalier, of Marvell against Lovelace, obscure somewhat the deeper rift occurring in the Western mind. To the new empiricist, the *philokalos* would insist that there is a complex mystery to existence beyond weight and measure, however finely tuned the instrument or mathematics. To the Cartesian gnostic, who removes consciousness itself from an engagement with any reality other than its own self-awareness, he insists on the actual existence of the created world, an anchor to reality around which blossoms beauty. The words of empiricism, nevertheless, became bent upon reductionist measure—*fact* as equal to *thing*—leading science at last to its cul-de-sac which Berlinski castigates in *Black Mischief*, out of which particle physics now tries to lead it. Berlinski finds Newton the source of the mechanistic simplifications of existence that increasingly trouble modern scientific disciplines. I suggest the causes more complex and anterior to Newton. The words of the Cartesian gnostic, on the other hand, submit to philosophical nominalism, leading to mind's divorce from all existence save itself.

I am speaking metaphorically again, using Bacon and Descartes as figures for a larger complex in man's new war with existence that we call modernism, a war spanning the centuries at least from the fourteenth. As for the poet in these centuries, he takes it that the Baconian empiricist and the Cartesian gnostic enter into an uneasy collaboration at the poet's expense. Certainly poets of all degrees of calling, from the *philokalos* to the mimetic, come to that conclusion by the nineteenth century. The antipathy to poets from the new philosophers and new scientists leaves such a confused poet as John Keats seeing existence as "shadows numberless." Even his longing for the vision of the *philokalos* seems such a vague illusion that he can only ask at the end of that great ode which so well dramatizes the poet's journey since the Renaissance, "Was it a vision, or a waking dream? / Fled is that music:—Do I wake or sleep?" We have moved from the poignancy of Tristan as Fool to that of Keats as Fool. For the glimmer of Beauty which Keats saw flickering and guessed to be somehow intimately related to Truth he can believe at last only an illusion. Fortunately for the poet's sanity and his possible rescue, one of Plato's *philokaloi*—Gerard Manley Hopkins—sees not shadows numberless through which one is seduced into despair by illusions of beauty, but a pied beauty in things. It is a vision that reasserts the relation of existence to the Cause of existence, celebrating in the world's decay a beauty's shining forth. Hopkins sees a wholeness in the hierarchic members of creation, even in those members' indisputable decay:

> No wonder of it: sheer plod makes plough down sillion
> Shine, and blue-bleak embers, ah my dear,
> Fall, gall themselves, and gash gold-vermillion.

One might have suspected all along that Plato could not rule out all poets from the republic of souls. He is too much the poet himself. He has most conspicuously that gift basic to the poet according to his pupil Aristotle: the gift of seeing likeness in unlike things, the gift of metaphor and analogy. In my own view, Plato is one of the great poets in our tradition, in a line of descent to us through Dante to our own T. S. Eliot. He is the reflective poet who attempts to recover that lost unity of our consent to existence which requires both the *philokalos* and the *philosophos* to be persuasive healer of the restless, willful mind. With the aid of the lover of Beauty and the lover of the truth of things, one may be guided, ever surer, through the complexities of existence. And so that brings me by long circling closer to the gift common to the academic community, resident in the individual academic mind, to which we must look for a recovery of integrity in the academy. We have spoken of the poet as Tristan the Fool, a fool who speaks in the anguish of a lost vision, dramatizing in his anguish that hunger in us for the climate of eternal love. Mark and his barons are too much empirical at the moment, hearing the words only literally; and because the literal surface of the words is so foreign to the literal circumstance, they conclude that only fancy is afoot. At no loss for words, as they say, their fool in their view is lost from reality. Those words about a crystal chamber all compact of roses and the morning are very Keatsian, as we have implied. When spoken by the *philokalos* they point out our fallen world. The poet who does so most effectively is Dante, whose vision of a lost world is so darkly reflected in his *Inferno,* where one meets again and again beauty removed from substance, often through terrifying images whose terror in us requires at last the *philosophos.*

So long has the poet in us been denied that it takes a while to call him back into residence, as by now you are uncomfortably aware. Let me turn again, and finally, to a medieval mind, the second great academic mind after Plato, to conjure that poet in us a last time. St. Thomas as *philosophos* remarks the nature of human intelligence. In reality that intelligence is simple in its operation, like God—metaphorically speaking. But the mystery of its operation in pursuit of the truth of things leads us to explore it, by which action it seems stilled for the moment. By analysis we separate its activities. In seeing the parts of this divine simplicity, the intellect (for we are said after all to have been created in the image and likeness of God)—that which we recognize as simple in its operation—appears complex in its constituencies. Of course, the danger of such analysis—this turning of a part of our intellect upon the whole of it—is that we perceive parts which only by our faith as scientist or philosopher may be believed simple in operation. First this; and then, this; then, this—the discursiveness of analysis belies the very reality which discursiveness is turned upon, the reality of thought alive, in a seamless simplicity. Analytic destruction of existence is the fear Wordsworth has in mind when he attacks the new scientist as "murdering to dissect," but the risk of such murder is no less that of the *philosophos* than of the biologist.

St. Thomas as *philosophos* undertakes this difficult task, wishing to say the truth about the intellect without impeding the thing itself of which he speaks: "Although the knowledge which is most characteristic of the human soul occurs in the mode of the *ratio*, nevertheless there is in it a sort of participation in the simple knowledge which is proper to higher beings, of whom it is therefore said that they possess the faculty of spiritual vision." Now what Thomas speaks of here as the second and simpler avenue to an encounter with the truth of things is an angelic mode of knowing, a way Milton distinguished in *Paradise Lost* as angelic in contrast to Adam's discursive mode. But Thomas's angelic mode is one shared by Adam, in Thomas's understanding of man's intellect. Nor is the position new with Thomas, being a concern to Augustine and to Scholastics between him and Thomas. It is at least as anciently recognized as by Heraclitus long before these. It is also a mode as new as our own considerable explorations of mind's relation to brain, though Professor Harre would advise us that no one of any discretion would speak of it in relation to angelic natures. The analysis of this intuitive mode of knowledge is part of a number of intense engagements with the problem in books like Robert Ornstein's collection of essays by various hands, *The Nature of Human Consciousness;* Peter Medawar's *Induction and Intuition in Scientific Thought;* Michael Polanyi's *Personal Knowledge;* and Eric Voegelin's *Anamnesis*. The list invites extension, but must include the widely known exploration of Julian Jaynes, *The Origin of Consciousness in the Breakdown of the Bicameral Mind,* in which Jaynes explores analytic and intuitive thought in relation to the biology of the left and right hemispheres of the brain.

Earlier on, I was presuming to speak of this division of mind in relation to Plato's *philokalos* and *philosophos*—the lover of Beauty and the lover of Wisdom—implying at least that both callings are in each of us. I suggest now that both callings are in each of us by our very nature as particular creatures in creation and are crucial to the meaning we give ourselves when we speak of ourselves as human. Though one might use some or all of the works just named in talking of this relationship, and thereby perhaps give the argument something like a derivative scientific plausibility, I still find St. Thomas' distinction the more helpful. But whether using St. Thomas or Polanyi or Jaynes, one should of course prudently avoid any pretense of having fully measured the action of thought with mechanistic or speculative logic, for the mystery of our complex being envelopes at last any pretense of absolute delineation of finite being. That is the hardest lesson of all for the finite mind to learn.

And that is why, and where, the poet may on occasion come to the aid of philosopher or scientist. He knows that there is possible, at the literal level of technology through the latest science, a chamber all compact of roses and the morning. General Electric will light and air-condition chambers somewhat like Tristan's dream chamber for us if we wish. But the poet will yet insist that something yet remains, the fullness that is at once within and also beyond what we might call the GE full-electric dream. For that dream of science through technology is capable at last only of a chamber inhabited by man reduced from his fullness. The controlled environment makes a world that is necessary to computers. In that environment meanwhile, man continues a restless presence. The signs of our discontent are as evident everywhere about us now as they were for Odysseus in that magically controlled environment of Calypso's island. Perfection arrested, or so it might seem from the outside: The goddess Calypso, on an Eden island, promises that Odysseus will be forever young and she forever beautiful. It is Keats's dream as he looks at the urn, life as art arrested, yet alive. From the shoreline, though, we see Odysseus longing toward Ithaca, planning his escape. Life is larger and more complex, we are apt to discover, than perfection arrested. It is so at least insofar as we understand perfection as the precise realization of elegant, reduced universes, every instance of which (insofar as witness has been borne to them) proving much too sparse for man's restlessness, his continuing sense of homelessness no matter how much he is declared to be at home.

St. Thomas, then, sees our gift of intellect as sharing in a mode of simple knowledge which itself prevents our ever being quite at home in any universe which the rational mind may define. That is the mode such a rationalist as Peter Medawar—and for that matter, most of us—touches upon with a word like *intuition*. It is a knowledge stirring in us that cries out that all is not yet known. Heraclitus is aware of this country of mind when he, the philosopher, speaks with the voice of the poet, saying that in a state of receptive contemplation we find ourselves "listening to the essence of things." It is the state of the intellect in which, as Wordsworth recalls in "Tintern Abbey," one "sees into the life of things." If Wordsworth does not himself distinguish St. Thomas' *ratio* and *intellectus,* the rational and intuitive modes, with a Scholastic precision, his poem demonstrates very clearly his recognitions, dim but there, of a division of thought and feeling and of the desire that they be brought into accord, into concert. It is, as we have suggested, the visionary poet Hopkins who answers Wordsworth's unrest, embracing the transience Wordsworth locates in his own mind. Hopkins finds it rather a signum of an inclusive intransience, a Beauty past change which is only echoed in "all things counter, original, spare, strange," including even man's mind. Hopkins embraces this transience, as Wordsworth and Keats cannot, through a faith in his own angelic intellect, supported insofar as he is able to support it by that mode characteristic of the human soul, the rational intellect. Hopkins embraces the complementary offices of *intellectus* and *ratio,* to put it in scholastic terms. To put it in older terms in respect to Western intellectual history, he recognizes that as a single simple intellectual soul he is both *philokalos* and *philosophos.* And, of course, this is the very point intended when I said we must summon the poet back into a residence in the academic community by first summoning him back to an office within each intellectual soul in that community.

One could write a more considerable exploration of this concern. In doing so, he would surely discover that individual poets, from Homer to Robert Frost, are deeply engaged by the conflict between the *intellectus* and *ratio,* knowingly or unknowingly. It is the poet who is most likely to believe that those forces in civil war within him are intended to be mutually devoted servants of the soul when the soul is in good health. That is why perhaps Wordsworth asserts in his "Preface" to *Lyrical Ballads* that poetry is the first and last of knowledge, that the poet accompanies the man of science wherever he goes. That is why the critical problems of the "dissociation of sensibility" so troubled T. S. Eliot at the outset of his journey as poet, with the attendant problems of the "personal" to be controlled by the right "objective correlatives," so that through words the poet stirs recognitions of the truth of existence and the suitable response to that truth by both the poet and his reader at a level beyond the modernist sense of the "subjective." Aside from that poet's intense concern for a rescue of the person of the poet beyond his poetry, and beyond the merely personal, he dramatizes for us as well the conflict of *intellectus* and *ratio* as we may encounter it in society, thereby forearming us against the always threatening chaotic circumstance in society. The threat seems to have reached an alarming level in society's academic community, a level which C. P. Snow addressed as a disintegration of the intellectual community into *Two Cultures*. For it is sufficiently evident that those two cultures—that of science and that of the humanities—are cast as antagonists in our world, increasingly at odds. But the split, I urge you to consider, is first of all within the individual himself—within the soul divided against itself. That is a tendency in us through willfulness, exacerbated by a propensity common to us which some of us describe as Original Sin. In that division, the one or the other—the *ratio* or the *intellectus*—becomes increasingly withered to a vestigial remnant.

Only as we quicken those complementary presences in ourselves, and so in the academic community, may we expect to bring into equilibrium their extensions to the general community. Only when this begins to happen will we begin at last a recovery of that mystery of community of which St. Paul speaks in saying that we are members one of another, distinguished in our callings but—as St. Thomas contends—fulfilling each his own calling through the ordinate recovery of *intellectus* and *ratio,* or as the poet might and does put it, heart and head. Only then, I argue, may we begin to exorcise the "black mischief" in limited science, the arrogant usurpation of being by the *ratio* in each of us. And to be evenhanded in the matter, since the truth of things requires us to be so: Only then will we be able to resist the temptation to an escape to a crystal palace all compact of roses and the morning, beyond the reaches of any sickness in roses or any uncertainty in the morning. For that is the danger in the heart (the *intellectus*) when uncomplemented by the head (the *ratio*).

There is much much more to say, much more that I wish to

say on my argument. But let us return to our point of departure: I can at last only bear witness to my encounter with this truth. I cannot transplant it boldly into your waiting mind, however eager both you and I might be for such an operation. I can cry, "See! See!" But that is all that I can do, expect for this final, weak attempt at reassurance that the exploration will be worth the expense of spirit and mind.

The academic mind that I have spoken for and to, insofar as I have been able, is on every side besieged as none knows better than you. The temptations to abandon the concerns, for advancement, for instance (and how many succumb to the temptations of deanships); for comfort in salary or prestige; for peace of mind in the chaos of our community's mind—the temptations to abandon concern are great indeed. Those who have been long in the academy sometimes feel it a matter of obligation to post over its entryway as a warning to those seeking intellectual integrity that chilling inscription Dante encounters on the threshold of Hell: "Abandon hope, all ye who enter here." We feel in moments of incredulity, when the world about us is suddenly beyond adequate description in respect to the seeming randomness of mind in the academy, like crying out: "What is there in the list of strange and unexpected events that has not occurred in our time? Our lives have transcended the limits of humanity; we are born to serve as theme of incredible tales to posterity." We might notice, however, that these are words spoken by Aeschines in 330 B.C. In our wiser, quieter moments—when we see if briefly into the life of things—we might say with the French writer Charles Péguy, "Our mission is not to make the truth triumph, but to fight for it." Or we might say with T. S. Eliot that there is no such thing as a lost cause because there is no such thing as a won cause. And we might at last engage the risks of mind, even with some cheerfulness—as unlikely as that may seem—remembering additional words Eliot leaves us, words spoken in a unified voice of the *philokalos* and *philosophos*, the voice of *intellectus* and *ratio* in concert: "If the Temple is to be cast down / We must first build the Temple."

In my institution I have been sharply critical of the public relations attempts at self-justification and self-elevation in the interest of the community's largesse, the larger grants of public money to support a larger and larger institution. I have been particularly critical of my school's official insistence that its primary concern is with "new knowledge," a phrase I quote from our "Red Book," the official rules used to examine faculty for promotion. The effect of such a provincial understanding of knowledge has been an emphasis upon publication by our faculty and pressure for what is called "innovation" in its teaching. Such a fundamental necessity to education as that of knowing what men have said of this idea or this fact is either ignored or rejected by such a prescription of a university's relation to community. In the pressure that results, the faculty member struggles to survive by being innovative and original. He contributes to that flood of "research" that even large libraries equipped with the latest technology can no longer keep up with. Little wonder the faculty member, whose own contribution is supposed to be made in the light of what has been done on the topic in hand, cannot know whether he has made an original contribution to "new knowledge" or not. A colleague in philosophy tells me of a system in answer to these pressures for new knowledge, most difficult to discover in philosophy of all sciences. One submits his paper to a board of referees. If the paper is accepted, he is notified and the paper is filed away. He has an official title of a "refereed" paper to add to his vita toward that fateful occasion when promotion is decided. But even under this system, he will have had a larger reading audience than many published pieces enjoy. I have seen a study that reports the number of readers of a published chemistry paper to be 1.5. In chemistry, so I understand from news reports and from colleagues, the number of publications of research is so multitudinous that it has become impossible to know the extent of duplication in such "new knowledge." The expected savior, the computer, does what it can for those genuinely interested in the undetected duplications. But for the most part one has a field in which the illusion of a multiplication of new knowledge by faculty is maintained without question.

My criticism of the publish-or-perish syndrome, as it is called, baffles my antagonists, since I myself have published rather extensively, and sometimes see evidence that, unlike the typical chemistry paper with its 1.5 readers, I have as high as 2.5 and sometimes 3 readers, now that my children are older. I do not, of course, object to the publication of research papers or scholarly examination of the thought of Descartes or Heidegger. I applaud genuine "new knowledge," even as I remain confident that it is extremely rare in any academic field. My objection is to the perversion of words, and through them of minds, by forced publication, a distortion of legitimate ends by mechanistic and statistical measures applied to the young scholars, whereby they survive at what is an economic more than an intellectual level. Promotion committees depend largely upon the number of published pages, despite protests to the contrary, and upon a received opinion as to the current prestige of the periodicals in which these counted pages appear. The validity of the words published receives little or no attention in the counsels of committee. And so whether the words bear false witness or not gets lost in the procedural mechanisms.

What is more disturbing, because inevitably corrosive to intellectual health, is the effect upon the would-be teachers whose survival is put at issue at a Darwinian level. That many bear false witness is inevitable, even should witness count. Nor do I necessarily impute deliberate intellectual subversion, though young professors are like the rest of us—human and so capable of willful distortion. The reality is that, intentionally or not, they put the word at risk. Very often a prematurity of mind results in the wrong use of words. It is with that recognition in mind that a colleague of mine, reflecting on the flood of academic publications, especially from young faculty desperate for survival, remarks that these, too, are "children having children." There are certainly analogical relations between what happens at the biological and intellectual levels of community, in both of which the gifts of being are no longer generally valued. If there is a concern for pornography as a factor in the rate of teenage pregnancy and perhaps even in the violence of ordinary social affairs, surely that factor has tacit approval when community authority dissolves. There is, I suggest, a parallel pornographic industry in the undisciplined use of words, in this instance actually encouraged by academic authority. Given the decay of scholarly virtues, to put it bluntly, so-called scholarly publication becomes intellectual pornography.

New knowledge, let me suggest, reveals its validity in the light of old knowledge when old knowledge is held by an active mind. That mind casts a light backward to meet a light of mind cast forward by old knowledge, feeding the present infant flame—

the active mind—in whatever current intellectual night sur-
rounds that active mind. And any mind in any age is always struggling in that night. There is a symbiotic relation between old and
new knowledge, lifting and feeding and bearing the growing intellect. In this respect we might say that ontogeny recapitulates phy-
logeny. The discrete intellectual body—this particular mind—
is enlarged, advancing beyond itself. But see how easily one uses
the wrong word? "Advancing beyond" has tempted me to implications of the intellectual race, rather than my concentrating upon
the enlargement and fulfillment of the individual mind's dance in
creation. It is exactly such wavering in the academic authority
which casts "new knowledge" in the role of programming an
endless assembly line in the name of Progress. Thus academic
authority invests "originality" with a glamor and value beyond its
merits through an obsession with "new knowledge." That assembly line, in the daily round of community life, is a ratification of
acceptable signs—the concrete consumer products, already ob-
solete by the time they are taken up by the hapless in this super-
market milling-about that passes as life. This is the world which
we pretend to believe, with the help of a very active advertising
industry, a crystal palace all compact of roses and the morning.
But, of course, our restlessness gives advertising's "poetry" the
lie, though its poetry is a far more demonic sort than Plato imagined. For it is, with deliberateness to deceive, an imitation of a
decreed illusion, and not even a shadow of a shadow.

Society, community, is not a vast, infinite collocation of shelves
among which we wander, supplied by that factory we call the
academy, with its "new knowledge." Current pressures upon the
academy would make it precisely and only this. But our restlessness suggests that life itself is not an action of desperate pursuit of illusions posited as reality, to be encountered as we turn
into the next aisle. The perfect machine with its attendant ware-
house and outlets is not a suitable symbol for either personhood
or community, though such a symbol has its effective uses in the
control of persons and communities by the lords of power, those
whom an Eric Voegelin has revealed to us secular gnostics.

The way we may discover the truth about such illusions, in
the interest of our own recovery of being, is to be able to deter-
mine the validity of new knowledge about the truth of things.
That is why it is crucial to recover those lost tools of learning

which Dorothy Sayers recalls to us, tools which we shall examine presently. It is obvious that either new or old tools are needed, so that we may excavate this site where community collapsed, burying its mind. What is needed is a recovery of known but forgotten truths. In a philosophy department, that teacher who knows what men have said of virtue in all the complexities of that term *virtue* is far more important to the intellectual health of the student than a teacher who labors at situation ethics from an *ad hoc* present, thereby encouraging his students to suppose their own whims and twitches of mind to have the validity of sound thought. This is a specific instance of intellectual pornography very popular in the academy for a number of years now. But it is only that professor who knows old virtues—who knows what men have said of virtue since saying began—who can see clearly the possible truth or probable falseness in situation ethics. The adolescent intellectual, whether full professor or freshman, is at last capable only of thought at an adolescent level. In one way or another, he will be one of those "children having children," many of which offspring are destined to perish in the righteousness of time through a defective heart or brain or through malnutrition brought on by parental neglect.

Old knowledge, depending upon one's familiarity with it, will be dismissed as cliché, especially if one is inclined, as is Chaucer's fat monk, to "let old things pass," being much given to the new world about him of fine horses and fat roasted swans. But there are clichés and clichés. Once upon a time I spent much energy trying to demonstrate the meaning of *cliché* to my freshman theme writers. In our text, a Thanksgiving dinner table described as a "groaning board" was said to be improperly described because the metaphor was worn out. But my freshmen had never encountered "groaning board" before. It was as potentially fresh to them as any other description employing poetic device, poetry having been largely killed in them. A metaphor appears worn out only after one has encountered it almost endlessly and carelessly used, like the phrase in hundreds of short stories and novels where characters are eternally pausing for "a long moment."

In my attempt to rescue cliché, I have no brief for "groaning board" or "a long moment," though they might be effective as satire or for irony, requiring only the reader's recognition of them as worn out and their present use as playing with a common recognition between reader and writer. What I would have us do, however, is recognize and distinguish among so-called clichés. Some are not only valid but crucial, however much used and abused. What is more worn by iteration, we might ask, than "Two plus two equals four"? The phrase $E = MC^2$ is rapidly becoming tedious in these lectures. The grammar of knowledge—old or new—is by its nature inevitably cliché in that it formulates an elementary ground which we must share in order to encounter the truth of things. It is only when such elementary formulation may be assumed in our conversation that we are free to move beyond the seeming deadness of grammar, the weariness of the elementary. And the desire to move beyond the elementary itself requires our constant re-examination of the grammar of our conversation, since we so easily mistake or confuse that ground. If we fail to be responsibly committed to the elementary, we will find ourselves as community in a panic moment such as the current one. Our cry will be "Back to the basics."

The elementary ground, the grammar of knowledge, which we are likely to condescend to insofar as we take ourselves to be sophisticated, is more tolerable to the very young. For them, all the world is new, including very old words with buried histories. The literal surface of "Little Jack Horner" is a portrait of a seemingly inoffensive little fellow, quietly feasting. He is safe, just beyond the adult world, in which he would not be tolerated to fish in his plum pie. The story is quietly seductive in its music and in the teasing rhyme, and in the situation itself. As one grows older, he begins to wonder why Jack is in the corner and just what beyond the literal fruit may be meant by *plum,* since there is little reason for self-congratulation in finding a plum in one's own plum pie. Thus we may later rescue, or rationalize, our childhood delight by finding possible historical implications. Here, for instance, it has been suggested that the name is actual in history; one Thomas Horner, steward to Abbot Richard Whiting at Glastonbury Cathedral, was sent to Henry VIII with a pie in which was secreted deeds to twelve manorial estates. Horner, the tale says, took out the deed to the Manor of Mells, where his family has lived ever since. Abbot Whiting, with Horner on the jury, was convicted of hiding sacramental cups from the king's greed and was hanged, beheaded, and quartered. Or so runs the account in the Baring-Goulds *Annotated Mother Goose.* One notices the child's delight advanced to adult delight: The irony that Horner sat on the abbot's jury seems less history than art; the ascription of historical date seems off, more suitably likely to have been in the reign of Henry's father (Henry VII) than that of his more colorful son. There seems to have been some tampering. Here is a play in the making, caught in a nursery music with teasing overtone. That elementary ground to the basics of education, the grammar of knowledge, is here. Or consider the music of "Hickety, pickety, my black hen"—in itself an immediate delight, but it is a larger preparation as well. So we discover when we happen at last upon something like A. E. Robinson's line "Miniver Cheevy, child of scorn." The line echoes in its syncopation that older music out of the childhood of our language, out of the time of the Tudors; it becomes an effective signal that Robinson's whole poem is built out of clichés. In mimicking Miniver's arrested development, his refusal to accommodate old and new knowledge, Robinson makes a commentary on our humanity that enters the rational mind through the imaginative mind. Our response to Robinson, then, is a stage in our education that has been under way long before we encounter the poem itself.

Education in its preliminaries, then, is the labor of acquiring necessary clichés. In its advanced concerns, education is the assaying of cliché. For the cliché is a common coinage whose true value is obscured by the residue upon it from its having been handled many times and often abused in the handling. All language suffers such wear and distortion. But the mystery of language is that the validity of words, insofar as they are precisely oriented to reality, is never absolutely destroyed by use and abuse. A word may be mis-taken and so mis-spent because not fully assayed. It will nevertheless carry within it what it has to say about the truth of things. Aside from its intrinsic value, of course, a word may pass as coinage of quite another value, through general assent. Thus, if I should suddenly proclaim the virtue of *prejudice,* given the present surfaces of the word as we spend it most recklessly, I would ruffle sophisticated feathers. Then I should have to explain, by recourse to the depths of the word, that it involves prejudgment and that we live our lives out of acts of prejudice that are perfectly justified by judgment. It is such prejudice that makes me drive on the right side of the road or cross under a green light. It is such prejudice that makes it possible for me to set aside worry as to whether the stairs will be there when we leave this place. It is such prejudice that makes me more or less confident of my bank account or of tomorrow's sun. Without sound prejudice to depend upon, I should have to begin every moment of my conscious life as if there had been no moment of my life before this moment.

We use words, sometimes, at the face value they seem currently to have, not so much recognizing their value as recognizing the smudges given them by current transactions with them. Thus meanings accumulate in dictionary incarcerations of the word, bearing in such history the evidence of shifting prejudices, often evidence of a slippage between the signification and the signified. There is present, for instance, in the entry in the *Oxford English Dictionary* on the word *imagination,* a complex history of our understanding of man's place in the world and the role man plays as maker in the world, from the medieval understanding of the thing signified by the term *imagination* down to our own uses of this much worn coin. In freeing such a word from its present limits, seeing its full life in relation to mind, we discover in that word a most fascinating complexity, though much more may be revealed to us than we are prepared to accept. This is to say that we grow out of ignorance, out of an adolescence of mind, sometimes in proportion to our exploration of old knowledge— out of our recovery of subsurfaces in the clichés we so randomly spend. Let me illustrate the point by personal witness.

When I have thirty sophomores in a literary survey course write a paper on the imagery of the opening lines of Sidney Lanier's "Marshes of Glynn" in comparison with the imagery in the opening lines of Poe's "Ulalume," my primary purpose is to make sure each one understands what is meant by *imagery* in relation to words. I do so with the knowledge of experience which tells me that *imagery* is a green term to them, though they have heard it spoken of. It is in some respects an attempt as futile as convincing them that "groaning table" is a cliché, though it is a far more necessary task in its consequences to the growth of their minds. I am always arrested by the consequences of this exercise. First off, there is a vocabulary common to a given class, out of their immediate encounter with the world which differs from mine, though we are in the world at a coincident time. Theirs includes, for instance, the latest pop music and movies and television shows. Just as there is a common popularity in the naming of infants, influenced by current fascinations (read the birth announcements in the "Family Section" of the Sunday paper), so is there a more general vocabulary among those babies as they come into their language. We have come through the Shirleys and Scarlots and Jennifers. Next semester's roll will say what we have come to. But their papers will no doubt still be full of "in my opinions," our moment of history having so heavily emphasized as if a fundamental truth that, in a society of the autonomous (as opposed to a community of the dependent), every mind's opinion has the same validity as any other mind's.

What I then go on to point out to my students is that, though they use much the same vocabulary and are restricted by the assignment to examine precisely the same two texts, each of the thirty-odd papers is unique. Each is, more or less precisely, a revelation of the mind using those common words. Short of plagiarism, no two papers are the same, though the problem each addresses is the same and the evidence to solve it is the same. Nothing is likely to bring home the point that this range of difference reveals levels of personal accomplishment so much as to read aloud a good paper and a bad one. The conditions—the limits of the papers—are rather commonly perceived by the exercise itself. Those students who accept one tennis player as superior to another, having accepted the lines of the court and the rules of play, sometimes begin to see that similar distinctions are possible even in intellectual "games."

But what I am most concerned to reveal to the individual student is that, beyond these dissimilarities in native gifts of intellect and habits of diligence, there is a recognizable presence of his own mind in the paper. There he may begin to discover the limits of his own gift. Since those limits are not yet arrived at, within the recognition lies incentive and direction to a development, insofar as he will take up the point. Incidentally, he notices a conspicuous dissimilarity in the imagery used by Poe and by Lanier. He sees a common world separately taken through a common language by the two minds. He begins to discover the presence of a distinctly discrete mind in common language. And at last, if grace allow, he begins to discover a collocation of several minds in the words he takes to be his very own as he writes his name and date on the paper in expectation of my judgment of him.

There really is, then, a community of minds within the words he has set down, though he has set them down in such a way that they are as distinctly his words as the handwriting is distinctly his.

We go on from there to talk about the particular presence of Poe in his words, of Lanier in his. We may discover, by the end of the course, that having read closely a poem identified as by Robert Frost, one may take up an anonymous poem and discover it also written by Frost, or by someone imitating Frost. Individual papers identifying accurately Frost as the poet of the anonymous poem nevertheless vary considerably in the authority with which each student shows the point, a consideration which makes professional judgment a requirement. One does at last have to say that this is an A paper and this a C paper, even though each paper may have named the right poet. For, in addition to the fundamental concern of leading each mind to occupy its potential with authority, students' authority differs in degree, as does teachers' authority. As some poems are better than others, though all may be poems, some minds are better than others, though all are minds. Both the teacher and the student have a double responsibility: to the individual mind in its potential; to the community mind in its necessities. What is confusing, given our world's distortions of both judgment and the ends suitable to intellect, is a mistaking of *moral* judgment as implied in the student's A or C, a point I shall return to.

And so one wishes to believe that out of such exercise the point will have been made that mind is responsible both to and for words—that it leaves marks on the words it uses for good or ill. One strives to make clear that, in judging and in signing one's judgment, the only moral danger to the student so judged lies in his not discovering and accepting and working with the gifts that make him a discrete person. It is not easy to bring a student to celebrate his C in these days, when most have unexamined As and Bs, any more than it is easy to be certain beyond hesitation that one's own judgment as teacher in these matters is valid. One professes with a constantly justified—that is, re-examined—authority, but one must profess. And the inescapable ground of profession is a confidence that words well spent reveal the educated mind: That is, an active mind engaging active minds is the context of any labor suitably called "education."

The importance of such student exercises in my view, then, is to make clear to the growing student mind the importance of seeing and identifying and judging the various fingerprints that cling to this coin of the realm, that cling to words. To do so is to discover the multiplying presences that gather in words, the minds in one's words as potentially infinite as angels on a pinhead. For here we are on the border of a mystery in words: In the word lies the focus of community, a community independent of time and inhabiting the house of language. In words are such presences that in a very real and not fanciful way we become members of a company of minds. And here I mean *company*, not in its commercial sense, but in that sense we mean when we announce to our household, "Company is coming." There follows from such an announcement a cleaning and ordering of the house so that we may receive that company. That is what significant education must be most concerned with, the cleaning and ordering of the head and heart, into which place may come a various company indeed. Homer and Plato; Sir Isaac Newton and Albert Einstein; the Saturday politician and the Sunday priest. The list of invited and uninvited guests goes on and on. Among the marvels is that any invited guest happily attends. The danger is that uninvited guests may. And in a disorderly house, the disorderly guest is safest from detection.

In either instance, then, the authority is, and it should properly be, that of the host or hostess of heart and mind, the particular consciousness issuing invitations or leaving the door ajar for the surreptitious interloper. If one through neglect of one's own house makes it equally available to whatever guest would enter, many strange and curious presences will attend, some settling down to a parasitic existence which if unnoticed and uncorrected may eventually dislodge the host or hostess. For though it is undeniable that, as Richard Weaver demonstrates, ideas have consequences and that ideas enter the mind through words and are sent forth from the mind in words to wander in the world, those consequences may be either good or bad. For there are bad and good ideas no less than good and bad intentions. The consequences are upon the life of the individual mind and subsequently upon the community of mind. Even welcomed guests may bring unwelcomed ideas into the mind. That is a point I make by caveat against Plato's argument of the inevitable good to the particular soul from its education. The enlightened mind, he seems to believe, must be consequently a good mind, evil a matter of ignorance and not of willfulness. That is why, in resisting that idealistic view of the mind and its education, I have insisted that an educator can only teach what seems known about the truth of things; what men have said of virtue one may teach, but it will not follow that the student will therefore become virtuous, even when he makes an A in the course. Which brings me, in conclusion, to the insistence that, as each citizen of community must be responsible for his peculiar gifts so that he may become an ordinate member of community, so—and even more so, in the nature of his gifts—must the student be responsible for the ordering of mind and heart; he *must* be, so that he may receive wisely and well those guests both invited and uninvited who are eager and more than eager to attend him. Education is the preparing of the mind for the presence of our common inheritance, the accumulated and accumulating knowledge of the truth of things. Each according to his gifts, but each with a responsibility for those gifts.

III | Liberal Arts and the Spiritual Confluence of Community

In the beginning was the Word. . . . And the Word was made flesh.
—John 1: 1, 14

We find ourselves now gathered, not as a committee of the whole, but in semblance of a whole community for a common meal and conversation, even if by the rule of manner on such occasion I am charged to do most of the talking. I want to talk at last about community in relation to its proper education, appropriate since as community we enjoy the hospitality of our liberal arts college. Let us say that there is a happy symbolic representation of community gathered here—a several body, members one of another drawn by a common concern about the means and ends of formal education. We are variously students and professors and parents and grandparents; we are physicians and salesmen and housewives and all manner of callings. I especially hope that there are some younger than students here, some not yet consciously drawn into this community's membership. If so, you very young will be more baffled than your older brothers and sisters, parents, and grandparents by what follows. For even semi-formal lectures are likely to be either insipid or baffling, and of the two I'd wish mine to be baffling, fearing that it may in fact be alternately the one and the other.

That the youngest should be the most baffled is as it should be, given the order and proportion in creation. But such a faith in creation aside, one must believe that, with age, one comes to understand more and more. We older must believe this, since there is no escape of aging. We will not accept aging as a falling away, and you young will join us in this stubbornness sooner than you may think. Our faith in wisdom's relation to age is built into our idiom: We *are* young, but we *grow* old, and one does not grow without some enlargement. Even though body stops growth when we are young, as the latest evidence assures us, we must nevertheless grow with age, either mentally or spiritually. At least, this is what we old tell ourselves in one way or another. So then, you young, prepare to be baffled. It would be a sad day for you, and devastating commentary on your near and dear elders, if you understood more quickly than they, though it be granted you to run and climb and leap more quickly and sing more clearly.

In wishing the presence of the very young, do I wish to confuse them? You? Those of you who are eager for the last bite of sherbet, who already anticipate the relief of a favorite television program if only this strange man would finish whatever he is about so that your parents might make their mannerly adieus and take you home? Well, no. I value your presence here so that you may be a continuing lesson to your older brothers and sisters and perhaps even to your parents and grandparents. That lesson is about a crucial aspect of community. For we are all, at least for the next few minutes, brought together in a complexity of community by our consent—however reluctantly given. I, the neighbor from over the Georgia line, am made welcome. For this evening we are made members one of another, with all the complexities and confusions and discomforts attendant upon such an embodiment.

As a body, we may stand for a community larger and more inclusive than the limits of our gathering. Those who prepared our meal had to know how many of us. From experience they have learned to prepare enough and not too much for our festive pleasure. But the ways in which a community feeds more largely than its immediate members is a mystery beyond measure, as any theologian or philosopher will admit. So we here gathered stand for a larger body not literally here in body, a body whose feeding is the responsibility first and foremost of this college which has made us all welcome. We are incorporated into that larger body by mystery. The youngster devouring his meat and potatoes prompts his parents to say, "It's a mystery where he puts it." What is meant is this: My reason tells me a child consumes less than an adult; therefore I have provided x number of chops for this evening's meal. But this unreasonable child has eaten his and his father's portion. The food, much of it, will be incorporated, in the literal etymological sense of that word, into the growing child. But the manner in which we are incorporated into larger community is not that of the pork chops as they make the child larger than he was, for which we may wish to be thankful. For the mystery of this incorporation, to which learning is primarily devoted, is our own growth as we become a part. By being a part, thereby being greater? The language is that of paradox, not of contradiction, for the community, of which we are symbolic, is not limited by this present moment. We reach, therefore, both to our past and to our future.

Now if you youngest among us do not understand *what* I am saying, that is all right; what I ask of you is that you remember *that* I said something. You will remember that on this evening I talked strangely, an experience you shared with those older than you and closer to you than I. You may even come to ask your father or mother or older and (in their view) wiser brothers and sisters on some tomorrow: What in the world was that strange Georgian from Crawford talking about that evening—you know, the evening we got home too late for "The A-Team" or "The Bill Cosby Show"? And if they have been attentive and remember, they may say something like: He talked of high matters, family and community and of the relation of higher education in its responsibilities to family and community. For one's older brother or sister must speak such language in such a mode, lest you not realize them older than you. But again, they may not remember at all. And now for the older among us.

Let me make clear, or at least clearer, what I mean by community as opposed to, say, committee. I have a motto engraved in wood. It might better be engraved in marble and set over the entry to all presidents' and deans' offices. It has stood over my desk for many years, standing me in good stead often. It says, "For God so loved the world that He did not send a committee." What we are taught, or used to be taught, is that God rather sent his Son, who is, as St. Paul puts it, the head of that body of which we are ourselves separately members in that most resonant of communities, Christendom. A committee is not body in this sense. It is charged by its creator through an annointed chairman—the creator usually a president who sometimes thinks he is God, if you listen to committeemen—to accomplish a limited task through a consensus of its minds. The degree to which it is of divided mind, to that degree it fails in its special calling. Now committees are often inadequate to their problems because they tend to be all heads and little body. In universities and colleges in particular, committees tend to be anonymous hydras. That they are such is not solely their fault. By their very nature they are limited; consensus soothes every head so that it may speak as if one. We have interesting poetry as a result, if the poet be ironic. Sometimes innocent of the surrealism to which committees are given, we say that these selected heads speak through their chair, a figure Dante would have some fun with, especially in the *Inferno*. Little wonder that, in the popular experience of committees—that is, out of the community's experience—we are likely to decide that a possum or a platypus is an animal created by a committee.

Community is quite other, though we should acknowledge that on occasion even committees take on the virtues of community. That is, a committee may consent to the variety of gifts in its several members and thereby move beyond the timidity of mere consensus into an active life. Still, it is not community as family is, or as Due West, South Carolina, is a community of families in the midst of which sits Erskine College. We speak here of a creature quite different from the notorious or anonymous hydra. Let us look at family as community for a moment. By its very nature in nature, the family's members are differentiated, as individually we find our own body's members differentiated. A finger is not an arm; neither is it an eye. The one reaches, but not so far as the other, though the reach of the eye is in a mode quite different from the reach of the hand. Both the hand and the eye hold, but in different ways, otherwise we must grope blindly or see without touching.

That is a poet's way of talking about family. Let us put it less fancifully, though reality, as I argued earlier, requires the poet's touch if we are to grasp the truth of things. It is the mother and father who decide that John or Mary are now suited to go off to Due West to attend Erskine College, in order to grow. It is John or Mary who, in concert with their parents and with their contemporaries, decide that Erskine would be a great or, perhaps, a horrible place to go, whether in fact they do make the journey. For John or Mary either to go or not go may be his or her own blind groping, depending on the relative health of that body, the limited community of a family, as well as the particular health of the member thereof—John or Mary. Meanwhile, the youngest—

Timothy or Robert or Susan—is saddened to tears. But nevertheless Robert and Susan make undying pledge to care for the ugly old cat Margarine (ugly from the grandparents' perspective), and they will love and play with the dog Bobby Sue while John or Mary is away. I assume here the barbarously named nuclear family, and one of some size, assuming most particularly the virtues in such a body. A sign of this imagined family's good health, for instance, is the general consent to name the dog Bobby Sue, after Robert and Susan—to the amusement of parents, to the envy of older John and Mary, and to the delight of Robert and Susan. Off at Erskine, taking interest in metaphysical poetry, John and Mary might discover the delightful accident of their own names in old Margarine, thought only a name honoring its color till they have read the intricacies of John Donne and been lured into fancifulness.

In his *Transposition and Other Addresses,* C. S. Lewis has a passage on community, specifically that of the family, worth our quoting to throw light on my argument that the family is a community:

A row of identically dressed and identically trained soldiers set side by side, or a number of citizens listed as voters in a constituency, are not members of anything in the Pauline sense. . . . How true membership in a body differs from inclusion in a collective may be seen in the structure of the family. The grandfather, the parents, the grown-up son, the child, the dog, and the cat are true members (in the organic sense) precisely because they are not members or units of homogeneous class. They are not interchangeable. Each person is almost a species in himself. The mother is not simply a different person from the daughter, she is a different kind of person. The grown-up brother is not simply one unit in the class children, he is a separate estate of the realm. The father and grandfather are almost as different as the cat and the dog. If you subtract any one member you have not simply reduced the family in number, you have inflicted an injury on its structure. Its unity is a unity of unlikes, almost of incommensurables.

You will have noticed that, where Lewis uses the army squad, I have used committee to strengthen my point. For if a community is not all legs, as with the squad of soldiers, neither is it all heads, as with an academic committee. Both Lewis and I are, as you will also have noticed, hierarchists, a position I embrace without apology, rejecting community as either all heads or legs or as a truncated hydra-legged creature such as one finds inhabiting the mythologies that spring from ideological readings of community. With that aside, a word about Lewis's point that when a family member is removed the family sustains a systemic wound. At the immediate level of the family's reduction, as when John and Mary go off to college, there is immediate and very local pain to the members separately. Little Robert or Susan mopes about the house for days, toying with objects that remind of the lost member. Even the dog may go again and again to the door of an empty bedroom. Bobby Sue may actually be off her feed awhile. And however bravely Father and Mother reassure these forlorn members, even the father and mother feel the absence acutely. It is most decidedly an open wound in the family body for a while.

As for the grandparents, they most certainly will feel it, advanced as they are and so removed increasingly from a world loved, though they may share with the parents the moment's delight that the tape recorder is silent and there is less traffic on the family phone. As for the absent member, amputated and transplanted into a strange new body, the college class—well, how may one capture the confused happy sadness of that creature whom the professor of English or philosophy or mathematics finds fidgeting before him some cold bright September morning? All legs and no head, a brainless centipede. Such may be the professor's estimate of the class as a whole, while John or Mary feels very much a lonely leg unaccustomed to dancing with this new body. What happens, one at least believes possible, is that gradually the professor as head calls a complex body into an order. In time John and Mary and each of the other members discovers his calling as member differentiated. In some happy occasions, the class in English or math in the fall of a particular year becomes the class of, say, 1987, thinking of itself under that name and meaning by it a body severally called to community, constituting for its four years a creature called the class of 1987, until that new creature must itself fragment.

What I suggest, by way of enlarging upon community, is that the wound in separation of members, whether of the family or the class, is less critical than it at first appears. Back home, the missing member is still present in very real and abiding ways, even when the tape recorder is silent, having been put off limits to the youngest by order of older, now absent siblings. John is present, even when young Robert has the temerity to move from fondling sadly the abandoned basketball to practicing shots with it out by the garage. Mary is present, even when young Susan begins to nag about taking over Mary's deserted room. And the missing members, John and Mary, find themselves sustained in a variety of ways by that large warm body from which they have been removed. They sit before the teacher, wrenched from their accustomed ways, but those old ways still throb in them.

One trusts that John and Mary now begin to discover membership in a larger body, a body inclusive of the family they thought lost. For it is surely a principal end of education that a student make such a discovery. He begins to know how very present to him are ancient members of his family, as he begins to have intimations that his own life in community will reach down to those remote from him, even past such inevitable memorials as the twenty-fifth annual reunion of the class of 1987. Slowly he concludes that among those remote from him are not only his forebears, but those for whom he is a present agent, particular members who will appear only in time future. That is, he begins to anticipate a family to which he will someday be father and grandfather. And that is why I said at the beginning that I welcome the literal presence among us of the very young, as I welcome the very old. The middling old we have with us always, of course. Those are the young who think themselves older than they are, the old who think themselves younger than they are. And as we all, infant to ancient, are constituted members one of another for this occasion, so do we already begin to touch members now distant from us. Our father's fathers tie us to their fathers. Our children's children tie us to their children. In this last discovery we begin to live in a paradox gradually enlarged as our minds and hearts grow. Our very young are at once behind us and ahead of us, undeveloped members vested in our future. Our very old are at once ahead of us and behind us, nearer their fathers, but ahead of us in that they have already grown in ways we have yet to grow. We begin to understand community, one might say, in the light of eternity.

Community allows us, then, the abiding presence of both past and future. With that recognition, we may the more wisely devote ourselves to those ties that bind community. We may realize at last the most central concern and responsibility for mind in community, most central to us individually and in concert. And please note that I say *in concert,* not *collectively.* For I emphasize a resonant opera as it were: story, music, dance—a concert quite lost to any merely collective assembly. It is a responsibility to this resonance that ought to govern the offices and conduct of the liberal arts colleges in the larger community of man: Colleges are music and dance masters to the mind; they direct community, insofar as mind directs spirit, in a significant dance of life. Otherwise, we shall degenerate into a race in pursuit of life, which always eludes us. Then, as we know, life becomes a rat race.

And now, concerning those ties that bind us in community, and the role of mind in discovering and strengthening those bonds. We shall say something about the ends of the formal education of the mind through liberal arts. What is at issue, I contend, is the individual member's obligation to reach an accommodation with his inheritance, a more complicated action of mind than mind's mere statement of the obligation. Let me suggest that the proper end of formal education is to establish in the individual person virtuous habits of thought. Etymologically, this is to say that the end of education is a recovery of those habits of thought proper to mankind by the nature of his being. In a more limited sense as well, the end is to discover habits of thought proper to this particular person in relation to his particular gifts. Now the word *virtue* is not a very popular one in our day, either in the academy or in the community. It seems to struggle, under increasing difficulty, to survive even in the province of theology. Hence the necessity of a few old words on this very old word, so that we may relate it to the education of mind.

Virtue, let us say, is the term we apply to the quality of being in any creature in respect to its potential. To the degree that a thing fulfills its potential, we may say it possesses virtue. In this sense, virtue is the measure of a creature's having become what it is granted it to become. Thus we may speak of the virtue of a stone or of a cow or of a person—things that exist under the auspices of nature and ultimately, primarily and most decisively, under the grace of God, to whom at last all virtue is referred. Or we may speak of the virtue of a poem or an argument—the thing made by man's mind or hand, themselves to be referred ultimately to the Cause of all existence.

I would suggest here a corollary: Each particular creature, insofar as it shows forth the virtue proper to it, exudes a beauty which, when seen by man, captivates. By creature, I mean to include all existing things, cows or poems or persons. It is this signal of virtuous being, this beauty, that gives us a catch in the throat when we see a graceful horse and rider take a wall, the rider and horse so one in an action of being that the action carries us with it. William Butler Yeats catches the point in exhilarating lines, in a poem most appropriate to our concern, a poem called "Among School Children": "O body swayed to music, O brightening glance, / How can we know the dancer from the dance?" The beauty out of the action of being—that is what Yeats is responding to. That is what we respond to in the better sonnets of Shakespeare. For not all of his sonnets are beautiful, a point to be remembered since in praise of accomplishment, that which is good is singled out and lifted up.

Some of you may find this difficult to believe, especially if you happen to be facing a test in inorganic chemistry or biology this Friday: One's breath may be arrested by the same climate of beauty in the chemistry formula or in the configuration of nerves in a frog's leg. If you examine your own responses carefully, you will discover that you have experienced moments of exhilaration in quite diverse intellectual encounters. "Ah, I see," you will have sighed, whether in response to the life of an algebra equation or the vibrating meaning of a particular word in a particular poem. When you wonder sometimes, as sometimes you must, how your teacher can, year after year, go through a poem or the table of elements without being bored beyond endurance—since you yourself are bored at the moment—a probable answer is that he may be as engaged by the beauty of the thing as by its truth.

These experiences help us understand why one of our great schoolmen defines beauty as that which—when seen—pleases. Any *thing* is beautiful, insofar as it *is* in relation to its potential nature. We "see" its formal correspondence to the truth of its being through our intellect—and the pleasure of its beauty is a reward for our having truly taken it in, our having truly "seen" it, as we say. Eureka! Oh, I *see!* Wow! Our response is varied, though that to which we respond may be common. As we return again and again, we may well see more and more. (That is why good art is inexhaustible.) And so it is through our truly seeing the multiplicity *of* things and *in* the separate thing—including other persons, of course—that we are bound in community with being. I do not mean to say that we all see with an equal fullness of sight, or that we each see with the same clarity of vision each time we look. Only that what we see, truly see with our limited gifts, speaks an abiding reality. And so it is that, individually, we find ourselves moved as much in heart as in head by our discovery of a thing of beauty, even when that thing may be a theory in particle physics which, in relation to the thing the theory proposes, none of our senses may themselves approach. Finally, that is why, in this common gift of a response to the beauty of truth, we may help each other enter more and more into the truth—or at least help clear away obstacles to that entry. Even, let me say it again, when we are only being guided by the professor of inorganic chemistry into the wonders of sulfuric acid.

Our nature is such, alas, that we are often moved to see as beautiful that which is not so; or we see as ugly that which is not so in and of itself. I myself hold such confusions of our seeing to be the mark in us of what is called Original Sin by orthodox theology, an inclination exacerbated by willfulness which we are often pleased to justify, with a nuance of virtue misapplied, as the privilege of our free will. But one may pursue the problem at a level antecedent to theological metaphysics. The procedure proper to the formal deportment of the teacher is at just such an antecedent level, since the teacher's primary responsibility is to enlighten things, to remove shadows from things, so that the student himself may see them by a light partially his own. As teacher, one does not say, This is a truth which you *must* accept as a moral imperative, even when it is true that one must so accept it or else not see the truth. Nor does one teach inorganic chemistry as a means to prove the existence of God, though I suspect the beauties in that discipline indeed contribute to such proof. Teaching at the level of the liberal arts is not a programming of mind, though ideologies emerging in contention with each other these past two decades have tended to corrupt curricula in that direction, and especially through whatever liberal arts curricula remain in the academy.

It were better to say, Let us look at this thing—this formula, this poem, this idea—so that we may truly see it. Of course, I intend no implication here of that relativism which has sapped mind in this century. In the schools, relativism has been justified as situational—whether one means situational ethics or situational grammar. But to see a formula requires certain refinements of the eye: One must focus upon the separate elements and the properties of each. To see the poem presupposes some confident accumulation of words and syntax and so on in the ordering of the mind's eye. To see an idea requires its context, in respect to both history and logic. It is thus that one may come at last to see that these certain words are superior to these other words, in respect to what the words are trying to be—a sonnet or an argument or a description. And it is true as well, by the way, that quite often it is the student who removes shadows from the thing observed, his teacher allowed to see more fully by the student. Hence the complementary role of Aristotle to Plato. One does not become an Aristotle, however, by protesting, "Professor, I never heard *that* before."

When we see a thing truly, we are thereby responding to its peculiar virtue. If we were strict Platonists, we would conclude that one *must* accept the virtue of the thing seen formally, since all seeing is a remembering of absolute idea. But unfortunately, this strict Platonist has set aside our inherited willfulness, through which defective freedom we are quite capable of denying the truth of things, even when we truly see them. That is, the failures of our own virtuous becomings are more complex in their causes and effects upon our seeing than merely a failure to see intellectually. Nevertheless, the role of formal education—that is, the role of the liberal arts education in respect to the forms of things—is to bring the mind to an intellectual encounter with the truth of things. It will not follow that to know the truth is to be free, as the adage holds; that is, it will not *necessarily* follow, though in recognizing contingency in freedom we are not therefore excused from the obligation to pursue the truth of those things it is our special calling to know. To the question whether virtue may be taught, whether we mean the virtue of things or the virtue in the student, the answer must always be no. No, if by *taught* we mean *instilled* and made *effectively active*. What we may teach is what minds have said of virtue or what minds have

said of the virtues in particular things, in respect to moral conduct in the one instance or to the beautiful truth of the formula
$E = MC^2$ in the other. This is to repeat that the teacher may remove obstacles to a student's seeing; he cannot perform the act of
seeing for the student.

As individuals committed to perfecting the individual intellect
that is ours individually, as patrons of liberal arts education we
are constantly plagued by seeing only partially and incompletely.
We may see, through intense specialization, the part; we may see
vaguely the whole through unfocused inclusiveness. We see partially through untrained minds or through willfulness or through
some combination of the two. But in addition, we are prone to accept and defend a partial or a vague seeing as an ultimate vision
of the thing held in our sight. We are prematurely concerned
with the completeness, the fullness, of our seeing and are therefore prone to conclusion before conclusion is warranted. Our
world as it is constituted presses us to such conclusion. We must
be productive. We must be on our own. There is a whole complex
of these pressures, so that one appears foolish when he reminds
our world how long education takes. Plato was under Socrates'
tutelage for twenty years and more before establishing his own
Academy. Not that he spent twenty-four hours a day for all those
years listening to Socrates and arguing with him. It is rather that
he came to a sufficient fullness only after a long maturing, at last
comfortable in professing a pursuit of truth. What I could wish
the liberal arts degree to accomplish for its student, given that he
hasn't Plato's leisure, is the conviction in him that his education
is a lifelong action. Even so, we yet must provide him intellectual
training sufficient to that long journey of knowing himself in the
world. Along the way, he is not prohibited by that training from
career, from family, from the inclusive role of membership in
community beyond the safe memory that he is of the "Class
of 1987."

As for his professor, the pressures are no less, making Plato's
Academy an impossibility. A professor's intellectual growth is
programmed—by degrees, by academic rank—so that his fullness as a full professor may be only the spectacle of a fullness,
sign without substance. While I was a young instructor, I heard
one of our regents—for whom we now have a number of teaching chairs named, he having provided the money—I heard him

say that our institution would be great in relation to the number of Ph.D's on the faculty and that to insist on the faculty member's having the Ph.D. would work no hardship on the member since, in his words, "any number of jack-leg colleges now give the Ph.D." In that same climate of thought, the most recent president of that same school informed its regents that "the caliber and qualification of our faculty have . . . improved markedly. Sixty-seven per cent of our faculty has been here 10 years or less."

I cite such attitudes not to rebuke them specifically, though they are worthy of specific rebuke, but to indicate how confused our institutions have become in respect to the truth of things. One is rather certain that the quality and caliber of a faculty might be markedly raised by the presence of members fully developed in their callings, a fullness not possible by the act of stamping them degreed by a "jack-leg college" or by dismissing them from service once they have served ten years. Although Socrates received decisive student evaluations—not only at his trial, leading to his execution, but by his sympathetic student Plato, who established his Academy some ten years later—Socrates would be hard-pressed to gain academic rank as assistant professor in our world. He had no degrees, no publications, and no international reputation as philosopher—at the time of his death. Those considerations aside, when he reached the height of his intellectual powers he was already superannuated by our standards, beyond the mandatory retirement age.

This inclination in us to conclusion—to certify the value of a faculty by the number of Ph.D.'s or relative youth—while it leads to absurd difficulties, is nevertheless one of our more important gifts as human beings, when it is truly seen. (Another of our gifts, of course, is that freedom to abuse gifts, which is why this particular one becomes easily distorted.) What the inclination suggests is that we have in us a restlessness for conclusion, a hunger for a rest in a completeness. If we distort this appetite for the fullness of being by centering on ends that are limited by time and place—limited to the world—we shall have abused that appetite. That is, we shall have secularized any hunger for completeness by centering our attention on complete things. Even universities are not ultimate. We come to the full meaning of this restlessness very slowly and, as a rule, after many mistakes and wanderings from the path through seductions of time and the world. But when this gift of restlessness is moving us aright, we discover a fullness of the world, a completeness in that the world has a cause and is no accident out of the clouds of accident, as our secularist confusion tends to have it. In that new discovery of the old world, we increasingly realize a fullness in the little old world that is ourself.

This restlessness, let us hasten to say, is not reserved to the professional intellectual alone, to the members of a liberal arts faculty, for instance. It is in each of us by nature, and it complicates our membership in community, even as it makes that membership the more necessary. The attempts to specialize the restlessness, to separate it out of community and reserve it to educational institutions, have been all too quickly accepted by the general community. By the separation, community for a while has the illusion of its own rest, of a completeness, since it has dismissed its responsibility. It is only when shocked by some crisis that the community once more begins awkwardly to attempt a recovery of its gift of restlessness. It begins to see that the end of that pull toward rest does not lie in worldly perfections. At this point in our history the community has not yet seen a relation between the fact that Johnny can't read or write and the fact that relativism dominates our national spirit. Community begins to cry out for a return to basics in education; it turns angrily against the spectacles of immorality that are consequences of a political pluralism extended to the absurd limit of pluralism, an insistence that each citizen is a separate estate of the realm, sovereign and inviolable. Hence the fragmentation of community consciousness, out of which the violently confused response of community conscience. Hence the stirring sense of being lost in a dark wood. Such is the effect of our loss of ends proper to the individual as a being, out of which must come his ordinate relation to community as a member.

Even with all the dangers attendant upon this restlessness that is in each of us as a special gift of our special existence in the world, it is nevertheless the gift in us that encourages a pursuit of the truth of things. We reduce that gift by willfulness, or rather dissipate the gift, in part as a protest against our finiteness, that limitation that causes rebellion ever since Lucifer's fall from Heaven. When we begin to see our true way, however, we begin to see that only in the formal disciplines of the self, including

those disciplines of mind to be acquired through formal education, may we hope to find guides and safeguards, limits, to this
gift of restlessness, so that it may move us toward proper ends.
Formal disciplines inform—put form into—or, more properly,
move us outward from ourselves in such a way that we are formed
to and toward whatever potentiality we have. Thus only do we become "realists."

We grow. We become. We come to remember and treasure
what dead Socrates still says: It is better to know than not to
know. For knowing is the forming of our given nature as human.
The child's curiosity and wonder, we discover, is a clear sign of
ways to virtue in us. One hungers to know about dinosaurs and
photosynthesis and biochemistry, no less than about the human
heart and mind as those two aspects of our being are in spiritual
conflict in us. What we are required to be certain of is that what
we think we know is true. That is the point of the cliché judgment, old and trite to the modern ear, but a signal of that elementary old sense which we deprecate or discard: "It ain't what we
don't know that makes us ignorant. It is what we do know that
ain't so." In the terms we have been using, this is to say that human incompleteness lies in mistaking what one has partially
seen as the whole of our act of being, our act of seeing. It is the
prematurity of a rest for the mind's restlessness. Let me illustrate
once more out of my somewhat ancient experience with undergraduates, then, what I have in mind as the sort of movement
toward informing the self through formalities of education.

Years ago I used to teach young students rather recently from the
country, though now they all seem to be from Atlanta. Often they
were the first of their families to go off to college, as I myself had
been even earlier. They sometimes felt embarrassed by the remnants of their community that still clung to their speech, particularly to pronunciation. Part of that embarrassment was because
some of their teachers were not full of beauty as teachers, to put
it kindly; part was because of a snobbery in fellow students who
exhibited an unearned sophistication. Perhaps Grandpa used to
say *jine* instead of *join*. Some of these students still remembered
in very personal ways his *razor strop*. How much of their baggage of language might be tainted by such outlandishness? they
would begin to wonder. That was a haunting question to them.

Were they ignorant? Too often we confuse illiteracy with ignorance, and while some of those students were "marginally illiterate," as we now say of many of our college graduates, it was their
teachers and semi-sophisticated peers who bordered on that ignorance which makes one a provincial.

Cleanth Brooks made a fascinating study years ago that suggests country pronunciations a survival of Elizabethan speech,
an interest he has recently continued in his Lamar Lectures. In
that early study he used Joel Chandler Harris' very accurate
transliterations of black plantation speech in the Uncle Remus
tales. He also looked into documents of all sorts contemporary to
Queen Elizabeth I. He concluded that very likely, that courtly
and sophisticated man Sir Walter Raleigh said *watermillion* and
gwine—at Elizabeth's court. We know from the plays' texts that
Shakespeare's nobility say such things as "I holp him." Even
later Alexander Pope will use *join* to rhyme with *fine*, our own
spelling but surely pronounced *jine* in Pope's day. So my young
student's grandparent who said he was "gwine-a jine the army"
would have been understood by that highly sophisticated satirist
Pope, as he would have been welcomed to service by Sir Walter
Raleigh, whose name alone serves us as shibboleth for sophisticated courtly manners and art. If such was the pronunciation
heard at the Elizabethan Court in Shakespeare's day and in
highly educated circles much later, something more celebratory
than uneasy embarrassment is required of the young student
whose grandfather or grandmother had spoken with such seemingly outlandish pronunciation.

When one begins to see that this outlandish language is not
foreign except in a sense geographic and temporal, that it is
rather a sign of continuity in his heritage through time, he ought
to begin to feel quite differently about his fathers and grandfathers and their speech. It is not, of course, that I advocate a program whereby we return to such pronunciations, let alone am
I arguing for a language divorced from present incrustations.
When healthy, words are a developing medium incorporating
past history into present history; neither of those histories are to
be abandoned with safety. I have been told that Irish Gaelic continues alive in parts of Ireland. I do not know that the attempt to
recover that old language is necessary to Irish independence,
though William Butler Yeats and many of his contemporaries in

the Irish Renaissance thought it necessary. The continuing news out of Ireland and Northern Ireland does not seem to show it an especially effective ploy. And Welsh is at this moment championed with fierce militancy in Wales as the instrument whereby a nationalistic ideology might triumph. But Irish and Welsh seem more vital in the world of mind through John Millington Synge and David Jones than through slogans like *sein fien* or on Welsh signposts.

Of course, we are not so outlandish as the Irish or Welsh nationalists in these matters—as we would have it. But we should note the very concerted attempt to establish the flat Midwestern accent as standard American pronunciation for the whole country, against which many of us rebel. Businesses moving to the South have gone to some trouble to retrain the Southern tongue through courses and seminars, the justification being that a pragmatic efficiency is at stake. I am not fully convinced that this is the only reason. For we encounter a chauvinistic assumption of superiority too often, whether it be in the guise of a New York City provincialism or a Des Moines provincialism. I encourage you to approach such reformations with extreme caution, lest in the end a form be abstracted from substance in such "re-forms" no less than in other modernist attempts at the reformation of reality.

Meanwhile one increasingly encounters barbarisms dressed as standard. Everywhere one hears "aren't I," for instance. "Are I not"? The country *ain't* recognizes a shortcoming in our inherited language and supplies a solution; the cocktail party term *aren't* forces form, making spectacle of language. We must not, then, conclude as outlandish that which is rather natively viable—if our reason for doing so is merely the discomfort we experience with our native ways with words when we move into what purports to be sophisticated circles. To make such a mistake will bring us at last to such abuses of language as you may, with a little diligence, demonstrate to yourself, particularly from the language as used by those for whom language is a primary tool— television newscasters, for instance. Form misunderstood becomes dominant, obfuscating substance. The words sound high, they say little or nothing. And when we undertake to erase illiteracy using such an attitude toward language, strange usage of words occurs, gradually infecting even the most diligent of us as smog infects San Francisco. We may find ourselves amused by desperate attempts to say a real thing through form misunderstood. I have at hand an anthology of quotations from letters to a welfare agency:

I am forwarding my marriage certificate and my three children, one of which is a mistake as you can see.

The syntax is highly sophisticated here. Even the *which*, comic at first encounter, is grammatically correct, though its logic refers us not only to papers, but to actual children. Another:

In accordance with your instructions, I have given birth to twins in the enclosed envelope.

Another:

I want money as quick as I can get it. I have been in bed with the doctor for two weeks and he doesn't do me any good. If things don't improve I will have to send for another doctor.

From the sophisticated syntactical structure in these words, one knows these writers had schooling well beyond the third or fourth grade. If not that evidence in the words themselves, one knows it probable from the state laws that require attendance till one is sixteen. Once we have enjoyed the accidental comedy, we may wonder what such writing says about our educational system. What seems evident to me from these specimens is that in the training given, the teachers attempted to impose form upon habits of mind without correcting those muddy habits of mind as the necessary prelude. Word and sentence form is at odds with word and sentence matter, suggesting a formula approach in the teaching, which in turn suggests that the teachers themselves do not understand fully enough the relation of form to matter. From such speculations, inconclusive here of course, let us turn upward, toward the higher reaches of the educational establishment.

The penultimate officer of a major university, the vice-president for academic affairs, explains the appointment of another academic administrator in the university. The quotation is in a public announcement. It was first written, then set in type, then proofread, then published. It is not off the cuff. "Dr. ———'s work will supplement the university's extensive activities currently under way to attack black and other minority students with good academic credentials." It is unlikely that this academic officer would recognize good academic credentials if attacked by them. But consider the chief executive of that same institution, speaking to the board of governors: "The blueprint for this drive to excellence was laid more than a decade ago." What boots it to wrestle with such language at the freshman level if it is acceptable coinage in the academic realm among that realm's highest leaders? One spends long hours pointing out at the freshman level that one does not *lay* a blueprint for a *drive;* one lays a foundation for a building from blueprints. Anyone abusing language in this manner ought to be examined more closely by his governors. But then one realizes those governors hear in these words only something equivalent to "Wow! Look how great we are. There's Progress for you!" But words do in fact mean particular things; to use them this way is to bear false witness, whether one does so out of ignorance or by intention. It is an abuse that warrants remedial work in English and logic, especially when the words are potentially destructive of community, as they are when spoken by the chief academic officers. This president's words are nearer in manner to those written by a welfare applicant who pleads: "My husband had his project cut off two weeks ago and I haven't had any relief since." If the one amuses, the other ought to fill us with alarm.

My continuing argument is that the academy has as its chief responsibility the stewardship of mind through words; its responsibility to words is paramount, since it is through words that we maintain a community beyond the circumstances of time and place. We maintain a *communion* of members through *communication, communication* being the most popular word at this moment of history, in which moment the thing the word names is most elusive. Embodied in a community of rational souls, we are members one of another. But the embodying instrument is words. Words mean some *thing* or *things.* Because of an abuse of them, we may take it that they mean something quite other than what they themselves insist on saying. Welfare applicant or college president, each has a responsibility to certain precisions. Nor is it an acceptable appeal to say, as student or teacher or president, "But you know what I mean." Individually and in concert, we are obligated to hold our signs—our words—as the firmest possession and proof available of our humanity. We know this, whether this truth be shown by the child in a moment of

panic or delight crying out "Mama!" or by the logician perfecting
his syllogism, whether by the chemist or neurologist or particle
physicist who must, more demandingly than others of us, depend
on signs to approach realities beyond the senses and beyond the
machines that attempt to enlarge and refine the senses in his attempt to measure reality.

If words—signs—are so crucial in these ways, we must make
a final admission. Though words are the primary concern of
the academic community—from kindergarten to post-doctoral
research—they are the community's responsibility as well. That
responsibility cannot be transferred by quit claim deed to the
academy, with the expectation of a continuing profit to community. Language is in the keep of mothers and fathers and grandparents, through their relations with the world as various as to
dogs and cats and children and professors and college presidents.
It is a responsibility not only for our own words as we use them,
but a responsibility to actively oversee the use of words by those
to whom a professional responsibility has been delegated. If we
delegate that responsibility, and then abandon the responsibility
to see what the delegated agent makes of his authority, we allow
that agent to establish a professional concern in the matter which
may prove in the event something less than a truly professional
concern. How reluctant the ordinary citizen is to say that a professional educator's words are used to convey nonsense. But nonsense requires only common sense to detect it, as a rule; it requires
no doctorate in education or science to see in what measure
words fit the truth of things in the tendency of a particular mind's
use of words, even a highly specialized mind. A community re-
luctance, out of false humility, is precisely what has prevented us
so long from effectively raising the question whether educational
programs have failed us. When the emperor appears with no
clothes, we need not object to his going naked among us. But we
should not pretend that he is clothed simply because we fear to
acknowledge the obvious—for fear that we appear ignorant. The
use of words is not a specialization whose only authorities are
professors of English. If they were the only, I'd have jined the
army long ago.

What one is being sold—what he sells himself through such distortions of reality, whether ostensibly dealing with things like de-

tergents or a college degree that prepares him for the life-race through technological grammars only—is all too likely to be a mess of shadows. By the very manner of the selling we ought to see that we are being used; that we actually are, or are taken to be, in ourselves merely shadows without substance, sufficiently registered by statistical abstract to be fed into programs. We are assumed to be willingly moved and manipulated through spectacle. The premise is that both we and the world are, in Eliot's words from "The Hollow Men," "Shape without form, shade without color, / Paralysed force, gesture without motion." If we can add a certain wildness to shape, shade, gesture, we have a moment's illusion that we touch upon form, color, and significant motion. Thus in a world made dependent upon the agitation of our perceptions, newness itself becomes the shibboleth whereby our deeper restlessness (which I have urged as proper to us as created souls) is controlled and redirected to false ends. Our proper end is rest; we long to find our place in the concert of all being which Dante presents in that wonder-full section of his great poem, the *Paradiso*. But that desire may be perverted to an improper concern that any *thing* must be *new*, rather than to an acceptance of the thing as itself. We become addicted to a possession of the new under the illusion that through possessing the new we are reborn. For when we have lost our orientation toward those ends that give ultimate rest, when we have so distorted our legitimate appetite for being till only a particular brand of cigarette or soap powder or college degree seems to promise rescue from restlessness, we will have become self-made victims of spectacle, pawns in the flickering circumstance of a present moment that is unrescued from time. We become haunted by vague dreams of some future moment. In short, we will have reduced life to a desperate race to no satisfactory end, out of its proper perspective as a dance in creation.

I have, by implication and at points directly, attacked the stance of our educational institutions as they now exist, not excluding those professing themselves devoted to liberal arts. I have done so because of their participation in such distortions as I have just described. But I have also said that those institutions, willy-nilly, are delegated stewards of mind, their charge being proximately from the community. Since this is so, insofar as those institutions fail, the failure is not theirs alone. The relation between the institution as agent and the community as patron is quite complicated, but it nevertheless exists. The ways in which each fails separately and contributes each to the other's failure are multitudinous, beyond the limits of a lecture or even of several lectures. But I think I can make my case tentatively, not through marshalling evidence and facts but by pointing to a common attitude toward the mind shared by community and institution, an attitude we will each recognize in ourselves in some degree.

Let us admit that, being more man-like than god-like, we have come to prize our individuality beyond what reality will tolerate. *Individuality* I set aside from *personality* as *personality* is understood by orthodoxy, which is not the same understanding held by that very new science of the person, psychology. (See Jacques Maritain's *Person and the Common Good* on the distinction.) But in a contradictory way and at the same time, we find it necessary to reject individuality because it is a limitation of our being. What we must recognize here is that we deal, not with a paradox, but with a contradiction. The gifts whereby we think ourselves special—whereby we are most particularly what we are and thereby unique—are inescapably limitations of our individuality. The confusion whereby we think of *individuality* as involving absolute freedom, including the freedom to become whatever we will to become, is deadly to *person*—to personality—because it substitutes dream shadows of the self for the reality of the substantial self.

In community, we are quite fatuous about this confusion, suggesting to the young member of community, for instance, that he can (not may) be whatever he wishes to be. Anyone can be president or doctor or college professor or farmer. Thus we obscure an undeniable reality from the young person, but not for long. Let us state the reality: By being special, by being particular and unique and individual—by being a person—we are necessarily limited. The fullness of our being is implicit in our gifts, which conversely means that our gifts define and limit the extent of our potential fullness. Our gifts may not be multiplied by changing our "lifestyles." Even George Orwell's barnyard totalitarians know this, though they use the knowledge for private convenience, not for personal fulfillment nor for a public embodiment of the person into community. Some creatures, they say, are more equal than others. If the sign of that inequality is the number of legs one has, the absurdity of the criterion does not destroy the validity of the principle. The failure to acknowledge the gift of particularity, the uniqueness of each person's actual existence as a limit to his potential being, is the principal cause of most of the unhappiness in individuals and the cause of that chaos in society which prevents society from becoming community. It is an unhappiness, I regret to say, subscribed to by both the community and its institutions, both bearing false witness against the true nature of membership.

When, in the name of the reality of human potential—in the name of so-called individuality—we assure our young that they can be anything they wish to be, we engage in what is actually the diabolic. It is diabolic since it is, whether by accident or intention, a destruction of reality and the solicitation of a destruction of reality by the young. We hesitate to declare it diabolic, the more's the pity. Baudelaire remarks of such hesitations in us that the devil's most clever strategy in the modern world is to persuade us he doesn't exist. But acknowledged as diabolic or not, we witness the effects of such destruction of being at every hand. Though we shield our sight from it through a vaporous sentimentality, its effect is palpable in the withering of those discrete gifts in our sons and daughters. Anyone who teaches in public secondary schools or in colleges and universities, if he pause for reflection, will recognize at once that it is this distortion of actual existence, the denial of the particularity of gift whereby one is a discrete and most valuable being in community, that makes effective public education virtually impossible. He will recognize the confusion of morality with mind training, a pervasive heresy against reality which can have come to dominate community only with the academy's and the community's consent. A word then on this confusion of morality with education, of moral virtue with intellectual virtue.

In our community mind, as it thinks of the training of its youth, we have increasingly consented to an absurdity, the result of which is that the community now finds itself almost hopelessly lost in a desert of its own making. To put it starkly, we have come to equate moral integrity with the college degree. Institutions, in selling themselves, have made the most of this confusion. Success—so runs the position—depends upon preparation. Success in the world speaks the ultimate reality of the individual. Success as a sign of moral integrity is the most vicious Puritan inheritance we have kept and treasured, not willing to go behind our father's word on the matter. The viciousness in the proposition concerns Nathaniel Hawthorne in several of his fictions. In "Young Goodman Brown," for instance, a young man content to take spectacle for reality—the outer show as valid sign of inner being—is destroyed when he discovers of his own volition and by participation that the bright, neat, seemingly happy communion of souls in a little New England village is rotten at its core. The shock is beyond his powers of recovery, dependent as he is upon his own powers alone. He dies old but full of bitterness rather than full of years.

Such then are the dangers in the common climate of thought about our young, governed by a co-conspiracy between community and its institutions. The most immediate exorcism possible lies in our recovery of reality, especially the reality attaching to moral being. A consequence of the exorcism might well be our return to life as a dance. May I offer, in respect to this dance, since my figure here is drawn from G. K. Chesterton's book on Chaucer, the lesson as it is implied by Chaucer in *The Canterbury Tales*. In the "Prologue" to this great marvel in our letters, we discover two brothers on the pilgrimage, from which they will return to their separate callings in the community. That is, they will not wander aimlessly in the world beyond Canterbury. The one is by his calling a parson, the other a plowman. I say *calling*, not *profession*. The parson, having discovered his gifts along the way, is an educated man, no doubt having attended Oxford University. The plowman, having discovered his own calling, deals and delves the earth, enlarging its bounty. Chaucer's narrator says, in obvious praise of the plowman, that he

> hadde y-lad of dong ful many a fother,
> A trewe swinkere and a good was he,
> Living in pees and parfait charitee.
> God loved he best with al his hole herte
> At alle tymes, though him gamed or smerte,
> And thanne his neighbor right as himselve.

The narrator's praise continues for several lines. The point is that these brothers, each very separate in the peculiar callings of his personhood, are very close to each other. The parson is quite comfortable in the presence of this rustic, unlettered brother. They are complementary partners in the dance of life. They are, in the poetry of St. Paul once more, members one of another, ordinate parts of that body we call community. As moral agents in that community, they are coequal; each has discovered his gifts and has worked toward the perfection of his gifts, not in order to be ahead of each other in a race. They have done so in order to come to the fullness of being prescribed, prelimited, by the gifts of particularity granted to each by nature and God.

If we in our turn insist on making plowmen into parsons, we shall destroy both. If we insist, we do so out of vanity or out of confusions of intellect. Or we may do so deliberately, knowing the transgression but willing to distort the reality of persons over whom we exercise a control in order to establish worldly power— as when the president of an institution argues that size is an equivalent of value to entice public support and then for the sake of size woos plowmen into a pursuit of particle physics or biochemistry. That is the ruse whereby one declares that a university with twenty-five thousand students and fifty million dollars in grants is *ipso facto* a leading university. In the manipulation the terms *individual* and *dollar* lose the significance they purport to carry in relation to reality, to the truth of things. We shall long since have lost not only intellectual virtues in the process, but moral virtues as well.

Joseph Pieper, in his refreshing consideration of *The Four Cardinal Virtues,* says to his reader: "In this realm of virtue, originality of thought is of small importance—should, in fact, be distrusted. It can hardly be expected that there will be entirely new insights on such a subject." His words ought to remind us that, in our concern for the truth of things our own originality is properly to be at best a secondary concern. Whatever our originality, it will be what the future discovers in us and so may be left to the future's care. Unfortunately, our whole culture is against such delayed applause. We note that the advertising of products from cereal and soap to automobiles is stridently bent on convincing us of the newness of the product of the moment, its newness almost requiring of us as a moral imperative that we seize it now. Soap powder companies are even in competition with themselves.

Having come up with their own new product, they must assert it better than their old, without denigrating the old lest we suspect them in the new or they be left with unsold remnants of the old. After all, last year or last month they were insisting the old product the best of all possible powders, having demonstrated to the camera (or rather, *through* the camera) that the powder removes all horrible contaminants when added to water. It becomes very nearly as salvific as the Blood of Christ. Are your life-style garments washed in the suds of our lab? One could almost make a hymn to this originality-by-association.

The concern for originality, packaged as the "new," obscures the truth of our daily existence. We get tired and dirty and hungry; we need rest and refreshment. But such basic necessities, insofar as they can be presented as exotic concerns, seem to remove the daily necessities from a level of elementary, basic concern. The humdrum must be made exciting. To see the absurdity of such ads, turn down the volume of your television so that you see only the actions and hear none of the words, and watch the antics of grown people dealing with today's wash or carpet cleaner or dog food. The general implication is that no thing and very likely no person is authentic unless stamped with bold letters NEW. If you love your dog or your child, prove your love with this wonder- and vitamin-filled food. It follows that, insofar as we are patrons of the "new," we share by participation in these (spurious) qualities of newness, as if in sharing we ourselves exercise not only love, but originality as well. We are innovative when in the newest car. If the thinking is not valid, it is lucrative, as witnessed by the firm's accountant at the end of the business year.

The confusion lies in a manipulation of *newness,* a quite deliberate attempt upon appetites through stimulating fear and desire to a superficial presence in us. Newness alone is made to seem a particularity in being, a dimension of essence. To acquire it—the newness—is to transform our being out of its essential nature. The point at which fullness is seized by us is that at which fear is stilled (our neighbor's response to our envy) or our desire gratified in the new product. Thus the "new," being unique, becomes our savior. Through it, we are set aside, lifted up. What one objects to in this manipulation is that in such confusion a valid concern for things is distorted, a proper spiritual inclination in us warped—with our consent—from its proper ends. The English poet David Jones has written a very great poem about the inclination, a prophetic poem in which he attempts to recall us to known but forgotten realities. It is called *The Anathemata,* which title suggests the lifting up of things in a votive way. And here *things* means all of creation, taken individually and particularly. That would mean soap powder and shirts and dogs and dog food and flowers and all of God's creation, severally and together, insofar as each is taken up by us, in and for itself, and in proportion to the world and to the Creator of the world. We note that *newness,* or our own *originality* in pursuit of newness, is quite beside the point of the "beingness" of such things, their existence as they are. For the genuine newness of existence lies in existence's being momently sustained at a depth beneath the powers of our finite existence.

Jones's comment on his title is worth our quoting, and indeed makes a sufficient rubric under which one might pursue a proper, vital, and viable education in the newness of creation seen in its eternal setting. Of *anathemata,* he says the term describes

the blessed things that have taken on what is cursed and the profane things that somehow are redeemed: the delights and also the "ornaments," both in the primary sense of gear and paraphernalia [soap powders and washing machines, for instance] and in the sense of what simply adorns [the child's colorful T-shirt, one's blouse or necktie or hat]; the donated and votive things, the things dedicated after whatever fashion, the things in some sense made separate, being "laid up from other things"; things, or some aspect of them, that partake of the extra-utile and of the gratuitous; things that are the signs of something other, together with those signs that not only have the nature of a sign, but are themselves, under some mode, what they signify. Things set up, lifted up, or in whatever manner made over to the gods.

The passage, I am certain, is as rich a rubric as one could desire to govern the ends of education, and I have forced myself to refrain from copious parenthetic illustration. But indulge me at least to point out that our delights at the Poll-Parrot stage of our lives, when we mimic creation in tribute to its very existence, are rich with the mystery of this highest deportment toward creation of which David Jones speaks. Things to a child are indeed *blessed things,* each in itself, requiring no composition of things in relation to each other, no ordering in the hierarchy of being. It is that moment that Chesterton describes when he observes, "A child of seven is excited by being told that Tommy opened a door and saw a dragon. But a child of three is excited by being told that Tommy opened a door." The whole of our life, once we pass through this three-to-seven period, is spent in one way or another in attempting to recover that lost moment, though we eventually confuse the end toward which we struggle—a recovery of the lost capacity for awe in the presence of reality—with condominiums or cars, positions of power, and the like. In this restlessness lies the secret of that conditional law given us: that unless we become as little children, we may not enter the kingdom. We ought to add, however, that—given our fallen nature—we do not become child-like through remaining childish. That is why the recovery of the child's visionary encounter with things requires a long journey toward a second childhood, a journey I think necessitated by Original Sin and, except through special grace, requiring a development of our particularity through the perfections of that peculiar thing we call the mind.

David Jones's words describing his term *anathemata* say a great deal about sign, about the importance of things like words in relation to the holiness of things like *Tommy* and *doors* and *dragons*. The passage is oriented, not toward originality or exclusiveness or uniqueness in that mind or spirit which is given to the lifting up of things, but to that mind's and spirit's seeing the truth of things—to its seeing the fullness of being in things. The fullness of which I speak is not a primary gift from the seer when he mistakes himself as originating being. That is the most general heresy in our world. But in Jones's words, we are most properly concerned with being, with essence—not with spectacle. Above all, we must not be seduced into a concern with a shadow, pretending to supply it substance by the authority of our own intellect. The disoriented mind, when it confuses its own encounter with existence to be the cause of existence itself, must inevitably be caught up in a panic hunger for a perpetual newness, caught up by the seeming necessity of the imagination's endless making of a world for its fleeting respite since consciousness is now lost from the existing world.

We see the point of difference quite clearly, it seems to me, in our misuse of the sign, our false witness in words, in the currently popular fad for "life-style." The suggestion in such a term is that we *are* through the signs we make; we mistake ourselves to be the very sign, rather than understanding that the sign is but a signal indicating what we are. The names we have must always be properly anchored in our essential and particular being, shining forth from that being. But in a distorted line of thought, as when we think ourselves to be the same as our "life-style," spectacle becomes all. Thus the emptiness of shadows must be what we come to and are in the end. We say facilely that we can be whatever we wish to be. The method we would use to become the wish is to change our signs, our clothes, of the moment. We therefore put on a "new life-style," the words of that phrase revealing how pathetically lost we have become among the rich wonder of creation.

If we are no more substantial than our gestures, no more real than our "style," then T. S. Eliot's characterization of our world as inhabited by hollow men is depressingly accurate. The chances of our rescue back to our essential selves, and thence to membership in viable community, are slim indeed—slimmer than those svelte ladies in magazine ads and television commercials who suggest that we are chic if we light up a Virginia Slim or that we experience something very like a sexual act with Homer's Calypso when we buy a particular new-model automobile. To see ourselves thus, so runs the seduction, is to enhance our "life-style" exponentially. "You've come a long way, Baby," says the ad, treating us as literal babies. In a world which increasingly confuses shadow with substance, the true virtues of things in themselves are confounded by vague biological desires, in a perversion of love. Thus one is well reminded of the remark we cited from Chesterton: Up to a certain point in Western Christendom life was seen as a dance. After that point, life becomes a race. We have outrun ourselves toward vaporous goals, a line of progress disoriented from the circular dance. But, Einstein to our rescue, straight lines have a curious way of turning back upon themselves. Our attitude toward the self and toward the world has left us alienated, separate, lonely—outside any comforting sense of community that orients us to a body dancing in tribute to *anathemata*. One who is ahead of his time, advanced beyond his fellows, must be inevitably alone, the price one pays for a reckless pursuit of newness or of originality misunderstood. When that separateness is taken as superiority, when one takes his position on the line of Progress as being at the cutting-edge of time, and when such a reading of the self becomes the primary principle of his existence, he will begin to discover increasingly that he races among shadows with shadowy competitors.

The proper end of formal education, over which the general community must keep a wary eye, is to establish virtuous habits of intellect in the student. As with any summary statement that would speak to the heart of a complex matter, this one needs expansion. I should like to enlarge upon it by first recalling that, in definition both ancient and valid, man is in his being at least rational animal. If we take that Aristotelean definition as it was baptized by medieval Scholasticism, it follows that the student is a spiritual creature, unique in his nature from all other creatures under Heaven. At least he is potentially so. It may well be that we observe exceptions among students and adults alike, seeing some we are reluctant to affirm spiritual creatures. But that is only a partial observation, exacerbated by our disappointment.

To speak of potentiality in such a spiritual creature is to suggest that man develops as he lives, and we have elaborate readings of human development from Shakespeare's "seven stages" of man down to the latest scientific descriptions. In relation to the question of how best to develop man's education, however, I think we might with considerable profit recall the Scholastic's reading of our intellectual development, the old view of our growth from green to salad days of the mind. Proof that we have at least a residual recollection of the old view I have in mind is our calling elementary schools "grammar schools," though that is almost the last vestige. Perhaps we still pay some obeisance to that old idea in some of our language. As we said, we speak of ourselves as *being* young but *growing* old, thereby arresting youthfulness with nostalgia. I suspect that when we speak of our "growing old" we think of age not so much as a maturing of the potentialities in us as a falling away from the Eden of youth.

Nevertheless, there is in such language a trace of the older truth about the nature of being that we may yet recover. We do still admit to reaching a maturity which we don't declare incompatible with youth. We grow old enough to obtain a driver's license or to vote. Thus we still debate the question of a sufficient maturity, recognizing some progressive stages, despite the concerted efforts of would-be educators to obliterate all such distinctions between child and man. For we are given to endless distortions of reality in the name of education. For instance, we have sixth-graders imitate in miniature the United Nations; that failed adult body is mimicked by eleven- and twelve-year-old diplomats who have yet to acquire an adequate control of their subject-verb agreement. And there is that insidious species of confusion of youth and age, of relative emptiness and relative fullness of potential: the reductionism whereby the teacher is cast in the status of child symbolically—the teacher's desk and lectern set aside and the teacher reduced to a membership among equals in a circle. The suggestion is that, since teacher and student are equally people, they are equally accomplished in their personhood. You may supply your own illustration from actual experiences with your own schools no doubt, since the deconstruction of education has been under way for a very long time, and none of us is likely to have escaped it.

But let us turn from lament to remedy, to those stages in the development of the potentiality in persons through education that may yet be recovered. Here teacher, parent, the community at large have vested interest no less than the student, who himself is likely to discover in old age that as youth he was robbed of his intellectual birthright. He begins that discovery when he gets to college and learns that there are such niceties in the use of language as subject-verb agreement and clear pronoun reference. Dorothy Sayers, the great Dante translator and marvelous writer of mystery novels, has an essay called "The Lost Tools of Learning," which ought to be standard fare in the training of teachers and of the teachers of teachers. In the essay she recalls the medieval educational trivium, a hierarchy of procedures in the training of mind that moves from grammar to dialectic to rhetoric. She observes how tellingly that system dovetails with observable stages in a child's developing awareness, his growing unrest in the world, as I have called this common inclination in us. These stages in what our day would designate the psychological development of the child she names as the Poll-Parrot, the Pert, and the Poetic Ages.

The first of these, the Poll-Parrot stage, is that of an insatiable drinking in of the world, a stage when undifferentiated observations are got by heart, as we say, with deeper metaphysical implications to *by heart* than we sometimes notice. At that stage the ordinary, healthy child absorbs nursery rhymes, along with the peculiar gestures of parents at table and parents' characteristic phrases. He absorbs fairy tales and the names of flowers. It is that stage in a child's life that we speak of, behind cupped hand: "Remember, little pitchers have big ears." He absorbs the world's wonders in general, with an appetite like that with which he consumes cookies and Kool-Aid. This is that stage when the multiplication tables and all the names of the pretty kings of France and England are meat for young minds more readily than they shall ever likely be again, despite those complaints against learning which the young mimic. The child is natively capable of the grammar of things here. Names are absorbed with great delight and boundless energy, if my experience with grandchildren this past summer was as it seemed. This is a period when falling leaves are butterflies, when apples come before apple trees. It is the time in the child's life when he makes those arresting observations we intend never to forget, but usually do. This, the grammar stage, when a truth of things is taken into the mind at the most elementary and direct level.

The second stage, the Pert, is much given to what seems at first incipient rebellion to the parent, which is why grandparents are so necessary to the sanity of the family as to a community. Grandparents are apt to know that more than rebellion is under way. Nevertheless, this is the age parents think of as the age of impertinence. Manners once imitated in mirror fashion at the Poll-Parrot stage now have to be repeatedly decreed with stern authority. Now, as Miss Sayers notes, the delight shifts to puzzles, conundrums. There is especially a great delight in exposing contradictions and gaffes, the more delightful when discovered in adults. If names are the matter to feed elementary hunger at the Poll-Parrot stage, the delight now is the yoking of names, that linking creating deadly weapons in the Pert mouth. "But *you* are. . . . *He* is. . . . *They* are the most. . . ." The verb complements here I leave to your memory, suggesting as a beginning of a long list *wrong* or *stupid,* as in "But you are wrong. He is stupid." You will also remember the subterranean uses of linking verbs reduced to auxiliary and yoked to active verbs, so useful in obscuring agency: "They are allowed to watch television till ten o'clock," which translates to "You are, as parents, both mean and unenlightened, while our friends' parents are not only enlightened but generous and loving." A difficult stage in the growth of mind, this one. Not only inevitable, but a present sign of potential health, despite an exasperating impertinence.

The final level in the awakening and growth of mind Miss Sayers calls the Poetic. This is what parents refer to as the "difficult age," in which the self-centered creature "yearns to express itself; it rather specializes in being misunderstood; it is restless and tries to achieve independence." With good luck, Miss Sayers adds, and with good guidance, it shows the beginnings of creativeness, a reaching out toward synthesis of what it already knows in relation to what is yet to be known. It is a stage beyond impertinence, but it employs both the dialectic of the Pert Age and old absorptions of the Poll-Parrot Age. Of course, the ages are not discrete nor exclusive, nor are they in any way strictly confined to biological development. In addition, their overlapping feeds each the other. And one inclination may be more marked in one individual than in another, degrees of intensity of each suggesting particular capacities in particular souls. One encounters grandmothers and grandfathers who exhibit an uncanny capacity as Poll-Parrots, for instance, in competition to get on game shows; one discovers an arrested Pert stage on Sunday noon news programs, like "Face the Nation," or at presidential press conferences. The Poetic stage surfaces in ideological activists in our time, their rhymed slogans overriding the grammar and logic of issues at hand.

I am wary of facile categorizing, and have not intended to be guilty of such a practice in what I have been saying about Miss Sayer's tools of learning. What seems valid here is not a rigid separation of stages, to be determined with reductionist studies by biologists or psychologists. Common sense, in relation to common experience—the experience of parents with their children and in tandem with recollections of their own childhood—suggests that such inclinations are in us and that they tend to be more pronounced at certain points of our development, from our merely *being* children to our *growing* up. Miss Sayers remarks that we may see in the child's growing personality certain stages that correspond in complementary ways to the hierarchy of the ancient educational trivium: "Grammar to the Poll-Parrot, Dialectic to the Pert, and Rhetoric to the Poetic Age." What I would wish to add is that those stages suggest a governing pattern to educational structures that we used to have. We continued those historical structures with the passive continuity of habit, but lost their anchor in classical epistemology, so that at a convenient moment, having forgotten the sources of the habit, we abandoned the structures. Since the Renaissance we have jettisoned the medieval grounding of education. Our principal "Poetic" ideologues have worked to do so—the self-centering effects of Miss Sayers' Poetic Age have resulted in a fragmentation of community and the emergence of sects around central ideologies. I must myself speak poetically here; what I have in mind is the sort of fragmentation of community through polarization that enters with Descartes on the one hand and Bacon on the other. The fragmentation one might describe as encouraging a divisive gnosticism: out of Descartes, self-consciousness centered on ideas as the absolute, the world of nature being taken as illusion; out of Bacon, the world of nature taken as absolute, with consciousness increasingly relegated to the level of an illusional effect in a material world. In either direction lies the secularization of spirit, of course. These concerns I have pursued in four or five books and so only touch on them here, but they are integral to any concern for the restoration of order and virtue in viable community.

And I must touch yet again on these concerns, since they bear so directly upon our argument for the liberal arts' responsibility to the student in his learning virtuous habits of being. When the individual has integrated his person, has realized an integrity of his complex potential, when for example he has established an ordinate relation in his mind among grammar, dialectic, and rhetoric—in response to creation—he will the more effectively contribute to an analogous reconstitution of community which has sustained an accelerating fragmentation since the thirteenth and fourteenth centuries. Of course, what I have been saying about the lost tools of learning would seem more appropriate to an immediate concern for elementary and secondary school education, as indeed these tools are. But I am painfully aware of the difficulties facing the liberal arts teacher at the college level. Now he is faced with teaching grammar first of all—the grammar of language, history, science. Some of my freshmen think the War Between the States occurred in the 1930s—I mean this quite literally. Some of them try to parse *like* in their own sentences as an element in standard syntax: "You know, like he's my father, you know and like what am I going to do about this?"

Our higher education, then, is largely given to the necessity of supplying the student with what he should have been given much earlier, which in some instances he *was* given no doubt but declined to possess. If we should ever reach a point of courage in academic expectations where a student is denied college entry on the basis of his elementary grammar accomplishment (I include math and history along with language here), we may be very much surprised by the salutary effect on the student himself. Of whom much is expected, from him is much sometimes given. Meanwhile, the failure of secondary schools to provide the tools of learning or the student's failure to acquire those tools in his classes has led our textbook publishers to limit the language in those texts intended for the college students to what they publicly acknowledge to be a high school level. Tenth-grade reading level is the rule for college text. The concerns of elementary education are very much the concerns of the college, which as of this present has not dealt with those realities though acknowledging a pressing necessity to do so. Evidence that we know where the problem lies is the endless number of basic texts, each with what purports to be a new approach promising miracle cures that don't occur, and next fall another new text, like endlessly revised soap powder. The promotional literature from publishers to professors sometimes reads like the pleadings of a preacher at a faith healing, as if by immersing himself in this particular text, or by the teacher's dunking him in it, the student will be cured of his disease. Meanwhile, our graduating seniors reveal much the same weaknesses in their use of language as one sees in the entering freshmen. We publicly lament the marginally illiterate college graduate, and not simply those out of athletic programs. Indeed, were the teacher's expectations of the student in regard to his intellectual development as direct and realistic as the coach's expectations of his player, we might have a significant renaissance of learning in the academy. The tools of learning on the football field are anything but forgotten.

We are very actively engaged at this point of our educational decline in "getting back to the basics," as we put it, a necessity with which I am in some sympathy. But that movement has my sympathy only insofar as we get back to the basic at the proper point in the individual's development. We must return to the concerns of grammar at the grammar school level. We shall be able to do so only through recognizing the basic nature of mind— mind as a gift in nature and most particularly a gift in human nature for which there must be individual and community respect and expectation. It is too late to teach sixth-grade grammar to college juniors. The restlessness and irritation expressed by such students over what seems merely a carping insistence that subjects and verbs agree or that the War of 1812 was in the nineteenth century or that inorganic chemistry differs from organic— that restlessness is at least in part because the eighteen-year-old is long past the stage in mental and biological development when such occupations for the mind are inviting. Why do I need to know this stuff? Alas, the answer from the college itself tends to be: Because if you don't learn it and have it down on your record you will not graduate and will not get that job you want which will provide you the condominium and Porsche you think you want.

Most liberal arts colleges, separately established or as constituents of larger universities, know in their heart of hearts, and sometimes even in their heads, that they engage in remedial grammar, though the course be called Algebra I or Western History or English Composition. They must continue that recognition, for that is the reality—that is the truth of things educational. We must do so even as we continue high expectations for liberal arts education. Such remedial labor is the only way we may proceed in the circumstances of a decayed system, though alone that procedure is merely a rearguard action in defense of a community life now largely lost. We teachers meanwhile dream of a time when we shall be able to address the concerns of the quadrivium at the undergraduate level, to turn to those subjects for which the trivium ought properly to be prelude. We know that, insofar as the old liberal arts quadrivium survives, it does so at the graduate level. The fortunate student with a master's degree may have accomplished the goal proper to the undergraduate A.B. As college teacher, I have quite willingly taken part in the labor of the trivium, even at the graduate level, in the interest of the student's reaching at last some fuller level of his mind in the quadrivium. I will continue to do so.

But I will also continue to insist that it is inappropriate to teach grammar school matter at the college level. If we may not blink the reality in our circumstance, neither may we neglect the necessity of improving the circumstances, lest our only role be that continuing rearguard action in a lost cause. That would be heroic action in itself, of course, and to be applauded and cherished, even if recognized only by a shrinking patronage. But it would not be the sort of additional labor called for whereby community health in matters educational might be restored. We know that high school degrees do not signify high school competence, that bachelor's degrees do not certify an undergraduate education. That is where we start from.

I recognize exceptions to my judgment that college degrees bear false witness. In particular, private secondary schools have come into existence in recognition of the general failure of public education, in spite of the political confusions that have treated them as spawned by racial or elitist concerns. If we are concerned at the public school level with getting back to basics, we owe more than is acknowledged to the private schools established in the past two decades for raising the cause to public consciousness. In these matters, we must not—as student, faculty, parent, alumnus—bear false witness. More importantly, we must not accept that false witness which is borne by others, however innocent of the truth of things those witnesses may be. We must the more actively oppose any deliberately false witness borne by those with vested interest, whether borne by the educationist who would maintain his control of public secondary education through specializations that are suspect because ineffective, or by the college president who would garner state funds by enlarging his campus and enrollment. It is time we stopped assembling young adults of grammar school accomplishment en masse to give them a high school education which we then declare the equivalent of B.A. or B.S.

So then, we must start with what is, deal with it as we must. We must call it by its name, loud and clear. Otherwise, we shall never recover the proper ground for proper education. We shall not get back to sound basics until we recover an understanding in the body of community of how the basics are vital in the development of those virtuous habits of being so necessary to the integrity of the person and the health of that body in which we hold responsible membership, the community. I hope I have made it clear that, while at times I've spoken to faculty, at others to students, at others to members of the community at large, I understand the responsibility to be ours together. Such are the current barriers to a sound liberal arts education, which I trust we may begin to take down—take down in ourselves and in our community, and most especially in those institutions to whom we have committed the life of our community mind. We must become, in this respect, intolerant. For intolerance, too, may be a virtue when understood as meaning an active resistance to nonsense or to sense wrenched away from its proper ends. We may not with undue charity accept an argument that a superior faculty is certified by whiskerless chins, that colleges or universities have possession of alchemical mysteries through which plowmen are turned parsons, that one may lay blueprints for drives to excellence, that new knowledge is the only justification of mind in the academy.

But we have said enough. Let us conclude so that the young whom I welcomed at the beginning may be gently waked and tenderly carried home to wait the morning's disappointment at having missed a favorite program, the morning's confused memory of a garrulus and tedious afterdinner speech, and perhaps a lingering savoring of the ice cream whose remnants disturb the aesthetic eye now and invite our impatient, kind community servants who must come after us and gather up our empty dishes. Tomorrow to fresh fields and pastures new—so long as we remember that fields and pastures fresh and new speak of a clearing made long before us by other laborers as dear and vital to us as the child we take home to a welcomed bed. If so, then all manner of thing indeed shall be well.

IV | The Quest for Community Ground: A Scholastic Foray

commuins (common): community, communication, communion, etc. The body of community exists. That is, it is a *res,* an actual "thing" quite other than, or separate from, or independent of, the *ratio*'s attempt to characterize it in verbal concept—including the present attempt.

The attempt to characterize *community,* setting it apart from all other "things" in creation by adumbrating the complex relation of the *idea* of the thing to the *thing* itself, inevitably results in reductionism, at the expense of the reality perceived and to the endangerment of the mind making an attempt at conception following perception. That is why, with caution and at the expense of tediousness, one must make careful preliminary observations about the intellectual act itself, observations long known but often carelessly forgotten. The reduction of the thing approached through reason is inevitable because of the limits inherent in the mode of knowing. Although the characterization or definition or description of any thing (in our present concern, the thing called *community*) is incomprehensive of the reality of the thing, we are obliged to attempt rational exposition precisely because rationality is the principal mode of our existence, distinguishing man from all other created things. If our rational pursuit of things is incomprehensive in its ultimate effect, it may nevertheless be sufficient to the establishment of a community of mind in things—*things* meaning all that we include collectively in the term *creation.* When that community is ordinately established, there is included in our awareness of it the realization that the inevitable reductionism that has led us thus far toward community with being (through *things*) does not affect the nature of things but only reflects the limited relation of mind to things.

The reductionism in the action of mind toward a thing lies in the mode of knowing and does not affect the thing essentially. A limit in the mode of knowing is reflected by the limit of concept in approaching the essential. That is why we must, having pursued the community of mind and thing as far as mind is capable of going, conclude only conditionally on the authority of "rational thought." The concept is *indicative* of the thing; it cannot *comprehend* the thing. For, though concept is a necessity in the mode of knowing named the *ratio,* the limit of that knowing is set by an inevitable distancing of the knower from the thing known. By the act of conceptualization, a distancing is necessarily effected. What this means is that the knower as rational knower is, or ought always to be, uneasy in that community of mind with thing because the community (a communing of) is always incomplete, interdicted by concept. A merely *rational* community with existence is insufficient to the mind's rest in community, though the very inclination to such a rest is constantly a temptation to an unwarranted conclusion that the union of mind and thing is *fulfilled.*

There is a desire to know beyond the limits of the *ratio.* And that desire is answered in a mystical, trans-rational mode of knowing, the experience of which is sufficiently common to us as rational minds that we not only accept that other sort of knowing but give terms for it and attempt to conceptualize it. That is, given an experience of a knowing beyond rational knowing, we attempt to "comprehend" rationally this added dimension of mind's relation to things, a relation which is itself trans-rational. Thus we speak of intuitive knowledge, of imaginative knowledge, of visionary knowledge, and so on. Whatever the nature of this trans-rational mode, whatever the degree of its comprehension of being beyond the mind's struggle to know rationally, let us speak of this mode with the Scholastic term *intellectus,* as distinguished from the *ratio.* It is a mode of knowing complementary to the rational mode and is that mode which answers the desire left unsatisfied when the knower has exercised the rational to its limit. At that limit, the knower knows his mind still separated from the fullness of the thing he would know, and thus he knows that his knowledge is incomplete. Yet he knows, though not rationally, that a fuller community with the thing is desirable, and he knows as well that he is not thus moved by a perverse desire. That is, he recognizes such a community to be the proper end to his own being in creation; it is a movement properly out of his own being, out of his nature and not contrary to his nature.

We have dramatizations of perverse attempts to gain this fulfillment of legitimate desire for community by illegitimate means, as in the Faust theme. In the persuasive literary developments of that theme, we should note, there intrudes the shadow of the diabolic, with the abrogation or appropriation of being by the *ratio*— as with Marlowe's Faustus, Milton's Adam, and so on. When the knower finds himself bordering upon a community with the thing desired, he may retreat into an assertion of the rational as absolute. But he may also open himself to possibilities of knowing in which the rational becomes—or seems to become—increasingly subordinate. That "romantic" inclination, which has been popular since Marlowe and Milton, *seems to become subordinate*, I say, meaning that when the mode of the *ratio* and the mode of the *intellectus* are *ordinate*, there is no *sub* appropriate to either. Insofar as the knower's action of intellectual being is concerned, the two have become one, are "married" into a transformed simplicity, as occurs in visionary moments.

One might make this delicate point somewhat clearer perhaps with the help of a prophetic poet. Dante, in *The Divine Comedy*, dramatizes his experience of this border country which opens him toward a final visionary moment at the end of his great poem. His pilgrim self (called Dante), the protagonist of his epic, has been guided through Hell by Virgil, who is the poet of the rational intellect, indeed the spokesman for the Scholastic *ratio* in Dante's poem. Virgil has repeatedly pointed out, often lecturing the pilgrim Dante, the relation between concept and manifestation, being particularly dependent upon Aristotle and even the Christian St. Thomas. (Virgil, though pagan, lives with knowledge of St. Thomas but without hope of fulfillment of that knowledge as is possible to Dante.) The pilgrim and his poet-guide emerge from Hell onto Purgatory Mountain on Easter Morning and as they move up the mountain through Ante-Purgatory and up Purgatory proper, Virgil continues his rational discourse on the truth of things encountered, as for instance in his lecture on the relation of Love and Free Will. But when Dante finds himself at last at the border between Purgatory and the Earthly Paradise and is confronted by Beatrice, he experiences a confusion of mind that makes him turn to Virgil for explanation. He discovers Virgil no longer with him.

In the moment before this panic-discovery, Dante has heard angelic voices singing a mingled hymn, *Benedictus qui venis* and *Manibus o date lilia plenis*, the Benedictus counterpointed by the passage from the *Aeneid*. This mingling of words and song occurs at the point where Virgil must turn and retrace his steps to Limbo. The elaborate pagentry that ushers Beatrice upon the scene confuses Dante, and he seeks rational explanation from his mentor Virgil, the rational poet. But what he is experiencing is an elaborate changing of the guardianship of his soul. Beatrice is to replace Virgil as Dante's guide for the final ascent into the mysteries of the Empyrean. There is a sacramental dimension to the pagentry through which, as Dante will soon discover in losing Virgil and the dominant *ratio*, he has not indeed lost the *ratio*. It has been lifted up and is enabled to go beyond those limited celebrations possible in Virgil, the Virgilian strewing of lilies at the gate of mystery (*Manibus o date lilia plenis*). Thus Beatrice, the "God-bearing image," replaces Virgil as Dante's guide. This is the point where Beatrice, the Florentine woman, is revealed beyond the limits of her particularity. As Dorothy Sayers remarks, Beatrice is "the particular type and figure of that whole sacramental principle of which the Host Itself is the greater Image." For this moment at least, Dante is indeed in tune with the world, for the first time, since in Beatrice is focused a new knowledge through which creation is seen to open upon the Empyrean. The mode of Dante's knowing from this point on, supported by the *ratio* still, is dominantly that of the *intellectus*. We have arrived at a point at which consent, the principle of affirmation, comes into its own, the point where the soul (in the poem, Dante's) enters upon a way to union with God. Here lies the way to that ultimate community with Being in which mind may rest at last. But it is a movement in which the modes of knowing appear reversed in dominance. The *ratio* now fully wedded to the *intellectus*, the *intellectus* moves the soul nearer and nearer to its desired fulfillment, more angelic in its mode of knowing truth.

Thus our point: The *ratio*, man's characteristic mode of knowing, as St. Thomas says, brings one to that uncertain country, at the borders of which the soul's openness through affirmation is crucial to the possible fulfillment of the soul's knowing. With the anticipation of arriving at this borderland (*repeatedly* arriving, we ought to say—since our journey within the world brings us again and again to the borders of this country), we return to consider that characteristic mode through which we may so arrive. We remarked initially that the *thing* we would know is prevented a full presence (save when grace allows us a "Beatrice" such as Dante's). That presence is prevented by the reductionism inevitable to the mode of rational knowing. We also remarked a danger to the mind should it attempt to command a full presence of the thing in community, by the power of its own will. One cannot will a full accommodation of "subject" and "object," as one might put it in terms popular to modern psychology and philosophy. It is the nature of that danger at which we now look, because modernist thought has so easily surrendered to that danger at the expense of its own further removal from the possibility of fully knowing existence. The rational mode of knowing is the distinctive mode to created intellect, to the knower man. Though concept tends to prevent a full knowing (a full experience of the thing by thought), concept nevertheless gives clear evidence of the real existence of the thing pursued—the actual existence of the thing as separate from the act of knowing it.

To the rational mode, there is a logical necessity of concept in relation to precept, aside from whatever *sense* (that is, perception) of the thing touching the rational mind. It is at this geographical and temporal point of knowing that the endangerment occurs, where concept engages precept. This is an action of back-formation in which concept and image are joined by the active mind. We are familiar with the sophistry (ancient or modern) that would deny the temporal-geographical context of knowing within which concept and precept are bonded; it proposes one species or another of solipsism, isolating the mind itself. But what we are less likely to notice is that other endangerment to mind (and hence to soul) through its won confidence in the existence of the thing, gained through its concept of the thing. For if the solipsist with obvious self-contradiction asserts his closed world the only reality (the assertion is the contradiction since it is addressed outward from the self), the rational intellect may at another extreme assume itself the final authority in relation to external existence—in relation to the thing known. That is, the concept may be taken not as *a* measure but as *the* measure of existence. Thus existence external to mind, while not denied, is easily mistaken as an effect of the measuring mind, owing its existence to that measuring. Mind may thus be tempted to rest the finality of being in concept. That is the most subtle danger to knowing, the most destructive relation of mind and thing, for it enjoys an illusion of community and not community, feeding our inclination to pride. That is why there is always the necessity of a *conditional* conclusion to rational knowing, formulated in words or manner (manners) reflecting that recognition. Such word or manner is an outer sign of a proper deportment of mind toward being other than the being of the knower himself.

This is to say that concept may too easily acquire not an ordinate authority but a pretense to an absolute authority in respect to knowing. Such is the constant danger in rational knowledge, a violation of the finitude of rational knowledge. The inherent desire to know, proper to the form of our rational being, moves the knower to a desire to comprehend absolutely, thus obscuring the limits of comprehension implicit in finiteness. For an absolute comprehension would "replace" the particular existence comprehended, while dissolving the finiteness of the knower. This "knowing" is not a god-like condition such as is suited to pious being but an attempt at God's own knowing. It is usurpation—or attempted usurpation—of the Infinite.

We cannot know a thing fully; that is an impossibility implicit in our finite existence itself. Nevertheless, we may know that the thing exists with a certainty separate from our comprehension of it. Thus what is rationally known is not invalid, any more than it is absolute. It is incomplete but sufficient to our nature as knowing creature. Thus, while our nature as rational being obligates us to a full pursuit of the truth of things, we are obligated as well to be mindful that knowledge we gain is not absolute knowledge. What is at issue in this distinction is that delicate balance in the knower necessary to the reality of his own being in its community with creation: What is described is that necessary piety of mind toward its own gift of knowing and toward the existence of the thing it would know, without which piety there will inevitably result a transgression upon being through the very attempt to know. That is, when the desire for communion becomes an obsession to comprehend, it has become ungoverned desire.

Something very like this attempt to articulate the piety of mind I take to be in Socrates' saying on the one hand that it is better to know than not to know, and on the other that he, Socrates, is the wisest of men (here citing the authority of the Delphic oracle) in that he knows only that he knows nothing. To know a thing absolutely—that is, to comprehend it, to absorb its being into concept—is an impossible fulfillment of knowing, though it is not impossible for the knower to be deluded into supposing it possible. It is against this supposition that Socrates sets his arguments. And we may repeat here that this illusion of comprehension is the condition of mind that agitates and energizes that secular gnosticism of which there is much talk (by me and by others). The supposition, the illusion, is necessary to gnostic thought in order that the gnostic mind may set aside the mystical field of knowing that enfolds a rational concept of the thing and the thing itself, the field (the ground) of community to which the *intellectus* is ambassador.

These preliminary reminders about knowing and its limits have been a necessary preparation to engage the theme expressed in our epigraph. *The body of community exists;* at an initial level it is a body of community between the particular mind and the particular thing. That is, community is a *res,* an actual "thing" quite other than, or separate from, or independent of, the *ratio*'s tendency to first characterize by concept and then take concept as absolute. Community exists quite beyond the rational measure or proof brought to the support of intuitive or tacit or visionary perception of the existence of that thing with which the mind has experienced—has enjoyed—community. It exists beyond the overt and explicit recognition of the existing thing (namely, the community of mind-and-thing). It is an immediacy of existence in which are bonded the knower and the thing, before the knower in some degree steps aside from that community in an attempt to name the known and bonded thing—the attempt to articulate that community, namely, the mind-and-thing.

In attempting to name this new thing, the *community,* we begin with as much rational control as we may command. Let us say: A community involves a coincidence of two or more things, effecting an addition to the being of each one of the things taken separately. Our principal concern, for which we have been pre-paring, is to say something fundamentally true of the community of persons, as a step beyond this initial community of the knower and a thing known. That is, we are entering upon a more com-plex concern in which the existing thing, a *community*, incor-porates thinking things in a more literal sense than at first one supposes; community in this sense is thus a *one* of thinking things—an embodiment of persons. A community in this sense, then, involves a coincidence of persons effecting an addition to the separate person's being beyond the discrete limit of person. Here the existing thing—the community—has dimensions of being that are at once engendered out of the particularities of personhood, but go beyond and are larger than the particularities of persons taken separately.

We may attempt to name this dimension by a variety of terms, depending upon the namer, the aspect of community he would name, and the like. Thus we speak of *collective*, a *group*, a *team*, and so on. In order to touch upon, or very nearly touch upon, the essence of community in its "thingness" let us name it meta-phorically, attempting an incorporation suited to the rational mind that does not radically violate the thing we would name. We seek the aid of that prophetic poet in whom the *ratio* and *intellectus* are the more fully employed in concert than in most of us: "For as we have many members in one body, and all members have not the same office; So we, being many, are one body in Christ, and everyone members one of another." Our poet adds that the gifts whereby we are particular member differ "according to the grace that is given to us" (Romans 12: 4–5). This is by way of remark-ing the particularity of being, the specific personhood of the dis-crete person. Again, "If the whole body were an eye, where were the hearing? If the whole were hearing, where were the smell-ing? . . . And if they were all one member, where were the body? But now are they many members, yet but one body" (1 Corin-thians 12: 17–20). (If we were to apply the remarks to our earlier concern for the relation of knower to thing, we might ask such questions as, If the *thing* were *concept*, where then were the *thing* and where the *knower?*)

Our prophetic poet, St. Paul, is explicitly remarking that Com-munity of all communities, the Church, toward which he exhorts us to strive in a pursuit of fulfillment of our discrete member being, a condition of full-bodied participation, caring one for another through a Love that sustains membership. His figure, let us note, is built out of that body whose love is the first of all our loves in the setting out, the love of the separate self. The self: that discrete individuated existence which we understand as a complex unity of hierarchic members. Within that discrete unity there is necessarily no respect of member as person, no respect of member as divisible from the unified body. This is a point of considerable importance to the metaphor being built by St. Paul. That is, while there is very certainly a structure of proper office in a several membership, there is no "class structure" among the separate members within the structure unless exercised at the expense of the full life of the body itself. One can imagine, for instance, a dictatorship of the *ratio* to an extent that the fleshly body is wasted, as in a scholar's arrest of his body by its incarceration in a cell of monastery or library. Nor may the self-evident hierarchy of structure in the body be denied except at cost to the body, for "if they were all one member [or if all members were *identities* of each other], where were the body?" What is common in this community of the separate person is a consent to the fullness of his personhood, to the body of his being. *Body* here is larger than, but not exclusive of, the chemical or biological or the like. There is an anarchy against that body, then, when foot would be hand, but also when *ratio* would deny hand or foot, absorbing all members through concept into a gnostic separation from the fullness of person.

We need here to dwell somewhat on *body* as that term is meant to represent the discrete, particular being. When we speak of the person as a body—*anybody, everybody, somebody*—we intend more than physiological or psychological being, even as St. Paul does. We are attempting an inclusive designation of personhood such as we also intend when we speak ordinarily of a person as "body and soul" or as when we say, attempting greater precision, that the person is that rational being existing through the substantial union of members of the body and soul (in which formulation *substantial* is a crucially complex term which denies the easy separation of "body" and "soul"). Unless we understand the complexity of *body* in the metaphor St. Paul uses toward describing community, we shall end up reducing community to the level of physiology and of psychology in our thus too limited sense of its being. The result will be an abstract paradigm as manipulated by the *ratio*. This has indeed been the procedure in the deconstruction of community since we began losing meta-physical anchor to our political and social sciences, particularly in those reductionisms of post-Thomistic thought.

Consider, for instance, the "science" of Hobbes, Hegel, Locke, Rousseau, etc., etc. With the rise of conspicuous effects upon the body of the world and upon the body of community in the world, effects exercised by the rational intellect through empiricism and Enlightenment appropriations of empiricism, the body of com-munity has been increasingly reduced to the physiological, re-moved from any mystical dimension of being; that is, the idea of community has been removed from the fullness of community body in its actuality. Community life is thus exorcised by rational analysis in the interest of various attempts to restructure that body. This is the procedure suited to the dimensions of rational knowledge when the rational is increasingly assumed to be abso-lute. We are speaking once more, of course, of the gnostic assault upon being, especially in its effect upon social structure, and we might take John Locke as exemplum. Locke is especially invit-ing, in relation to our larger theme, the pursuit of the grounds of community. This is so in the light of his address to the family as he poses family against political structures.

In the first of his *Two Treatises of Government,* Locke is con-cerned to reject the arguments for the divine right of kings. To do so, he rejects the family as a part of the structure of the po-litical community in order to get at the dominant metaphor that permeates the divine right principle. The analogy of the father-hood of God and the fatherhood of king is not so easily open to attack, for strategic necessities, as the fatherhood of king in rela-tion to fatherhood in the family. The procedure most amenable to the purpose at hand for Locke is to dissolve the natural ties of family to political structure and not engage too directly the super-natural ties. In addition, his *Second Treatise,* dependent upon a "Darwinian" logic of speculation, puts nature in a subordinate re-lation to political structure. It depends upon arguing family itself as existing at the natural level, out of which evolves a political structure that then sets family aside in the subordinate realm of nature. Thus in the *First Treatise,* family is argued to be consti-tuted of accidental configurations of blood and place. The relation of a father to a child is quite limited: limited primarily by time—family having been reduced to a point in nature at which the accidental configurations occur. But once the child arrives at a majority (whose definition is to be established by the political mind in the end), he is released from obligations to the family. He puts family behind him, as it were, entering upon the larger sphere of responsibility, that of the state. It is at such a juncture that, presumably, one moves from a state of nature within the family into a trans-natural social state through "contract." Rather certainly implied in the argument is that the "citizen" moves *beyond* family and is no longer a member of that body in a fundamental way but is rather member in the political body into which he is risen out of his state of nature. The confusions we inherit out of this disjuncture of family from the social and political structure of families plagues us still; they are confusions distorting our understanding of the meaning of community as we are building that meaning. (One wishing to consider the "Darwinian evolutionary" argument in social contract theory should read Willmoore Kendall's analysis of this Lockean deconstruction of family, "The Social Contract: The Ultimate Issue Between Liberalism and Conservatism," in *The Conservative Affirmation in America* (Chicago, 1963).

To return to our central point: Community exists; it is an actual being, however incomplete or fallen in its being. And it exists beyond any reduction we make through analogical language as we try (through metaphor anchored in nature) to name as actual that being which is present to our knowing, though it cannot be touched by the senses as a thing apart from the particularities that are its ground. When we speak of community as a "body" it is our attempt to make emphatic our belief in a reality out of actual experience and yet beyond the reductions of concept or simple category. Community is incipient to consciousness and opens the separate self to something beyond itself from the moment the self turns outward from the centripetal pull of self-centeredness. Community comes into existence through the encounter of mind with any other *thing* when the mind's action is governed by piety. That is, any *thing* becomes a creature and not simply a thing in the popular sense of the term, at whatever level of creatureliness it exists. Community is especially a potential consequence when persons encounter each other. This consequence is an event in experience even at a most elementary level, however fleetingly, as when strangers meet and only nod or when a passenger buys a newspaper from the boy on the corner. In such encounter, one senses the potency of community. Our manners, even at such an elementary display, are an acknowledgment of that thing *in potentia,* the community. Through gestures we acknowledge creatureliness other than that of our separate selves. Thus is the self bound to separate selves in an existence that is the ground of communion.

But we may discover more persuasively the existence of this community we pursue, and in an undeniable way, at a more complex level of coincidence of persons, namely, in that coincidence called marriage. Here conspicuously is that intimacy of membership beyond the complex of separate members; here one recognizes a body beyond membership. For when "two become one," the *one* is an enlargement beyond simple addition, a point most important to recall if we are to advance in our understanding of community in its social dimension beyond our inevitable reductions of formulation—beyond the always inadequate (if always necessary) attempt to say what constitutes community. For a community of citizens is not sufficiently a community when accounted for statistically or geographically, by the naming of its place and population count. Census bureau parameters of community are quite inadequate to reality. That is why, as we indicated earlier, a deadly blow to community results from John Locke's attempt to remove the family from the structure of community so that he may arrive through abstract speculation at a "science" of political structure deduced out of history and subsequently labeled, packaged, and sold as the "social contract."

Locke, in reserving family to the category of nature, denies the sacramental dimension of family which is celebrated in both marriage and baptism. If in marriage the body of a union is enlarged exponentially in respect to being, as the sacramental vows affirm, then the reality of nature itself is far other than understood by modernist thought since Locke. In baptism, that enlargement is sacramentally certified, a remark that requires some development. In marriage lies an experience of the mystery of transforming love. *Eros* is assumed into *agape,* enveloped and absorbed by *agape.* Contrary to the drift in understanding of this mystery since the Renaissance, *eros* is not exiled from that community of one, the sacramentally bonded husband and wife. We cannot escape observing nevertheless that a Puritan coloring of the concept of nature affects our general understanding of natural procreation; in the popular imagination "natural" love becomes set apart from "spiritual" love, with ardent defenders of each opposing the defenders of the other. That is, since the Reformation *eros* has been set at odds with *agape,* and it is well to recognize that the conceptual thought of Locke in respect to the relation of the family to the political structure is a source of that antipathy. I contend, of course, that it is a false antipathy, a consequence of distorted thought, just as the separation of the modes of thought—the *ratio* and the *intellectus*—and the pitting of each against the other is a consequence of distorted thought. The wars between romanticism and realism, between pragmatism and idealism, between art and science (the warring pairs may be multiplied) prove to be civil wars again and again. And they prove to have, again and again, their deepest roots within the separate person, having become internally factional, as it were. From that division in the person a distorted person becomes committed factionally to actions in community.

An accelerating erosion of community rises to historical notoriety in the 1960s and 1970s out of these conceptual antipathies. The youth movement of the 1960s, for instance, chose to emphasize eros as an aggressive act whereby to rebuke their fathers, whom they labeled the "Establishment." Their actions, as shocking as their imaginations would allow, but ultimately governed by the limited imagination of the Establishment (as is always true of actions primarily antipathetic), carried a message considered bold and conspicuous by the youthful proponents: "Very well— nature is as you say. But we choose nature over your 'civilization.' Your social order is sterile and for all the appearance of order, it but masks a confused agitation toward ends asserted by your sterile minds as desirable and so no doubt sterile ends. We shall stop to smell the flowers and make 'natural' love in the public square."

What those radical young minds sensed in rejecting the so-called Establishment was that the Establishment had lost anchor in the reality of being, though those young minds lacked a language and an understanding of the absence they sensed in community. Their response could only be that of antipathy, then, and so consequentially inadequate to any restoration, though not inadequate to the usurpation of power, that opposite of love. (Nor were they so "young" as they thought themselves, such antipathies to established power being very ancient in the annals of mankind.) With a sense of desperation, enlarging by feeding upon itself as does the collecting force of a South Atlantic hurricane, they resorted to a range of "Happenings," directed against the academy, the political and theological authorities, and so on. The spectacle of Happenings that centered on nature, we should observe, were actions directed against the body of the world, and at a most notorious level (that is, at a level fascinating to the professional media) were focused upon human sexuality. The range was from Woodstock to *O! Calcutta*. That the Establishment was scandalized by the rude insistence on celebrating the sensual, and especially the sexual aspect of sensuality, carries an inescapable irony: The sacramental dimension of the sensual (including the sexual) had long since been exorcised from the Establishment mind—or so it thought, since that dimension was actually only forced into an internal exile from community understanding. Nature itself was reduced by thought to the merely primitive, in respect to its life in the person and in community, as seen by Establishment philosophy and theology. Nature may be thus conceived as a condition to be transcended by gnostic virtues. One could do so by reducing nature to the level of mechanics, whereby ontological or teleological questions inherent in nature could be set aside entirely or used as instruments in the gnostic restructuring of being, such questions owing their very existence to the rational intellect alone. This is to say that nature, by which is here meant the complex reality of creation itself, was reduced from its living, sacral contingency in and to the soul to a primal dependence upon the finite *ratio*. In consequence, the ideals of social progress held by the Establishment mind could be about as inviting to the "young" as the Widow's version of Heaven to Huck Finn. The confusion, out of which one could but have ignorant armies clashing by night, lay in a war over concepts divorced of reality. To oppose a gnostic idea (the Establishment's reduction of nature toward gnostic social ends) by another gnostic idea (the youth movement's counter of reducing nature to the merely primitive, celebrated at the level of Darwinian beginnings) is doomed to a perpetuation of distortions of complex reality. One is faced with a false dilemma when required to choose either the Widow's Heaven or Huck Finn's Earth.

The "fathers" holding power in the 1960s and 1970s awkwardly defended order in the name of community, but theirs was a community understood largely in the light of "social contract" theory, a theory with no viable metaphysical structure to relate it to complex existence. Especially it lacked a clear relation to "nature," that amorphous term to which we have taken recourse in the desperation resulting from metaphysical dislocations of thought since the Renaissance. In such rootless ideology of nature, which sees the created world as a given but increasingly dissociated from the Giver, the private was artificially separated from the public. That is why, among other reasons, Nietzsche proved so shocking a happening in Western thought. H. L. Mencken took delight in exacerbating that shock by baiting the establishment as he saw it, primarily the Protestant religious establishment, which was conveniently given local body for his machinations: the South.

The phenomenon of the sexual made public, as in the "Happenings" of the 1960s and 1970s, might have been predicted as a consequence of the gnostic separation of *agape* and *eros,* a separation long under way in Western thought, culminating in that elevation of power in the name of love through Nietzschean thought. For in the end the truth of being will assert itself, though the assertion be in spectacles of aberration, alarming dislocations of community such as we experienced in the 1960s. Another of the ironies to be meditated upon is the subtle kinship between the organized happening out of a Nietzschean climate of thought that surfaces in Nazi ideology, with its effects upon the community of nations, and the seemingly spontaneous happenings that set generations against each other in the 1960s and 1970s. If one believe that body count may not be so decisive at an ultimate level as soul count, one might begin to move beyond the level of spectacle, or beneath the level of spectacle, in discovering those kinships. And when such a distinction becomes possible to us, we may the more seriously engage the dangers of the present war between false antipathies of body and soul, the battle lines perhaps more a matter of social convenience than of spiritual finality for the contestants. In this light, the current battle over such questions as whether sex education is an appropriate subject to public education might be seen in a new clarity, for that debate itself reflects an artificial separation of principles from reality by both sides. The confusions in that debate are a result of the deliberate intellectual deconstructions of family in the interest of social and political manipulation, but deconstructions long under way in Western history and not merely a development in post–World War II history.

Not that the Establishment in the 1960s and 1970s did not misunderstand the radicalism of the 1960s as the immediate origin and cause of the dispute. The misunderstanding was a necessity in part for its self-protection, for had that power structure looked too closely into the origins, it must in the end have indicted itself along with the 1960s radicals. We need to make a point about the term *Establishment* here. The radical opposition to the social and political structures of power in the 1960s has itself become the new Establishment in the late 1980s. Its ideology is entrenched in the social and political level of civil authority to an extent that we witness a new radicalism springing up against it, a radicalism reflected in the political activism of the Fundamentalist movement. In that stance by the current radicals (the Fundamentalists), there is a concerted opposition to the teaching of "sex education" in public schools. That program, it is contended by the current secular Establishment position, will provide a new order against social decay, solving such problems as epidemic teenage pregnancy. It is a program justified by the argument that the family is in disarray, has failed in its duties. The argument is largely made by implication, since to enlist the family as crucial element in the restoration of order would necessitate an engagement of the concept *family*. Such an engagement must prove destructive in its consequences to the current Establishment power because the conclusions would necessarily call in question the Lockean tradition upon which succeeding establishments have been dependent since the eighteenth century. One notices, for instance, that the term *parent* is a primary term of approach, confusing in that *parent* has been a term disengaged from *family*. The *single-parent family*, given its secular context, short-circuits the force of family in community, anchoring the problem by implication in nature and thereby suggesting that social order rather than family order is the proper solution.

That is one of the accomplishments out of 1960s radicalism not alien to Lockean thought, then, since it means that by a dislocation of parentage from the locus of family into the larger arena of "nature," parentage may then be manipulated in a restructuring of communal authority which thus bypasses that central role of family that we have insisted upon.

The Christian Fundamentalists' opposition to sex education in the schools is handicapped by its own loss of understanding of the sacramental nature of family in the order of nature. It is the same loss we suggested as sensed but not understood by the radicals in the 1960s. Sexual dimensions of being, if understood only at the level of "natural" dangers on the one hand or only at the level of "spiritual" dangers on the other, are doomed. The 1960s radical acted out of his intimations that in our natural inclinations there is a life which is denied by the sterile view of nature maintained by the Establishment of the 1960s in the interest of its sense of social order. The 1980s radical (the Fundamentalist) senses that there are intimations of the spiritual in nature denied by what he sees as essentially an animalistic understanding of nature, now being advanced by the new Establishment. That new Establishment (of the 1980s) is concerned to control nature in a social order decreed through manipulations of being that are no less gnostic than were those of the 1960s Establishment. In both radical movements—the youth of the 1960s and the Fundamentalists of the 1980s—there has been a haunting sense that roots have been severed. The moment's promising blossoms seem suddenly to wilt before one's eyes. The *whole* vision is lost, the only saving grace a continuing recognition of loss. The obstacle to that salvation of community through a recovered vision of the whole continues to be an inability to discover and name just what it is that is lost to community. And what I am saying is that a *whole* vision of love is what is lost: Eros and agape have been severed and disjoined. The lost "thing" is a love witnessing a fuller experience of the reality of complex existence—a love bonding us in community and thus attuning community to creation. Love severed becomes appetite for power, whether exercised in the name of agape or eros, or exercised at the level of personal or family or community actions.

The continuing battle, which we have illustrated with the symptomatic instance of the controversy over sex education in

136 | LIBERAL ARTS AND COMMUNITY

the public schools, is between one gnostic understanding of creation and an opposing gnostic understanding, both of which are
partial but advanced by advocates as if complete. That has been
the condition of our public attention to questions of community
order for a long time now, whether we look at the Establishment
of the 1960s or its replacement in the 1980s, whether we look at
the struggle over pornography or abortion. We remember vividly
the radical opposition rising in the 1960s—the "Youth Movement"; we are aware of the current radical opposition by Fundamentalists, or the "Religious Right," to effects out of the 1960s
radicalism. But the power held at either moment maintains itself
from a base that is subterranean in the institutions of order. Bureaucratic establishment, submerged and relatively inconspicu-
ous, wields effective power through what is, to the popular spirit,
a superstition centering in the *letter* of the dominant ideology;
the letter is icon worshipped largely out of fear. In the name of
such icons, present circumstances are said to require social manipulations, the manipulators contending for our general consent
to the institutionalized "letter." But as Gnostic forces contend,
the struggle itself reveals curious identity between and among
those forces.

In speaking of entrenched bureaucratic authority, subterranean in its operations on the popular spirit of our age, I mean
most certainly to include the media, the voice now necessary to
ideological contenders for power. There is considerable alarm over
the recent effectiveness of Evangelical television, the mechanisms for which have been established largely outside the dominant channels. Only slowly is it being realized that the Evangelical media movement, so widely lamented, is set against a
demonstrably secular liberalism which permeates the dominant
television networks, the large-circulation papers, and the large
academies. Whether in the newsrooms of CBS, NBC, or ABC, or
in classrooms of the educational establishment, or in the government bureau or department, the letter of presumed laws of being
are promulgated toward collective conditioning, toward reflexive
approval of the pronounced letter, and with an insidious effectiveness on the popular spirit. For we must recognize that the
battle is precisely for control of that popular spirit. We observe
at the upper echelons of power structures—at the level of highest executive office—positions actually taken counter to the en-

trenched devotions to the current letter in the lower echelons. It is a common observation that a particular officeholder is ineffective in executing his mandate because of the anciently established civil mechanisms occupied by agents beyond his powers to reform. Similarly, stockholders and presidents of media corporations (like voters and elected officials in the civil realm) are likely to differ from the entrenched media operatives upon whom they depend. And the dilemma permeates the academic realm as well. If this contention is valid, it points to the actual locus of the struggle for power over the popular spirit. It also suggests that any dislocation of an established power is a slow process short of cataclysmic revolution. Currently, we know the excited arguments about Supreme Court appointments, the excited concern a proof of this generalization. For the concern is for the long-range effects of such appointments.

It is through an attention to this level of the struggle for power that we discover the long history of gnostic forces operating upon community. The glacial movements have effects surfacing in spectacle from time to time, the outer show attracting our concern from the questions of inner, the deeply radical, causes. We might profit from recent rapid shiftings of spectacle, seeing that the gnostic force regnant in one moment is followed by a different gnostic force—at the level of spectacle and not differing fundamentally. Thus we consider whether the same glacial movement brings to the surface both the Youth Movement of the 1960s and the Fundamentalist Movement of the 1980s. Consider, for instance, that both depend from that most ambiguous of concepts, nature. To the Fundamentalist opponent of the rationalist view of nature, that view is out of a secularized reading of existence, nature understood as it has been largely understood since seventeenth- and eighteenth-century rationalism. That understanding has been certified in the popular mind by science, and by such pseudosciences as Darwinism, Marxism, and Freudianism. Hence the Fundamentalist attack upon "secular humanism." The current Establishment, against which the Fundamentalists contend, may properly lay claim that it maintains a traditional position, out of seventeenth- and eighteenth-century philosophy understood to have been certified by nineteenth- and twentieth-century science. Crucial to that philosophy, as exercised in community, are Lockean political ideas. For the tendency of traditional radicalism, given its intent to gain and hold power under a faith in man's autonomy, has been the rejection of all order except that decreed as centering in and originating with man. The refinement of Lockean political "science" personifies abstract *man* as an illusional *individual,* seemingly made concrete. Current confusions, celebrated in emblems like Feminism, Fundamentalism, and the like, are out of this mistake of seeing the abstract, the disembodied, as if concrete. The illusion of concreteness results from an infusion of the so-called individual's frustrations into the abstraction; it follows that the abstract letter will be seen as the inevitable container of the frustrations. And indeed, this is precisely the mechanism necessary to any gnostic control of the popular spirit.

The term *individual,* let us say, is for us a refinement out of the Lockean social polity. Through refined emphasis the "contractor" (the "individual") is encouraged to a decisive concern for himself over any concern for the body to which he is committed by social consent. But considered as individual, rather than as person, denatured being seems thus elevated beyond natural limit. One has established a principle with a seemingly transcendent aura, the rights of the individual. The alchemy lies in the removal of sacral being, of personhood. The effect to be observed, from traffic cases to trials for treason, is that *person* stands aside from the principle; the letter only is allowed as applicable to a circumstance in which an integer, an "individual," is on trial. The sense of one's membership, participating in body, is replaced by an allegory of individual contending with abstraction.

In respect to the philosophical perspective on this drama of the "individual" in nature, one has a simplified Platonism. It appears in our social actions, in two species, but species not fundamentally distinguishable. The one is the Fundamentalist's revival of the ancient Gnostic separation from, and rejection of, the full embodiment called *person.* Nature, and especially human nature, is rejected by a presumptuous transcendent leap which, though made in the name of grace, presumes an absolutist position in the very act of rejecting embodied—"natured"—person. The second species is discovered by its subscendent reduction of nature; thereby it would maintain an orbiting of nature by the action of its reduction of nature. This is the species called secular gnosticism, and in it one has, not the Fundamentalist's revival of that ancient Gnostic heretic's attempt at transcendence by a rejection of creation, but a secular angelism whereby nature is reduced by the absolutist intellect. The Fundamentalist would escape time and space as evil; the secular gnostic would control them as the means of siphoning intellectual energy, thereby elevating the *ratio* to its orbiting position above time and space. From that presumed position, it justifies its agency as cause of millenarian visions in the restructuring of being. Figuratively, the one looks up and away from being; the other looks down upon. But what is most disturbing is that they differ more in the *direction* of their flawed vision of being than in the flawed vision itself. If one does not truly see, it matters little whether one look "up" or "down."

It is in consequence of a kinship of flawed vision that the two species are blindly locked in the current struggle over possession of the perspective to be decreed, in self-mirrored antagonism. The one would require that all must look up; the other that all must look down. Since the arena of that struggle is the social and political one, the spectacle of the struggle is most conspicuous in our social and political affairs. Neither faction, let me suggest, is given to the recovery of personhood, to the reality of our beingness. And both increasingly advance the cause of the individual, in the growing eclipse by spectacle itself whereby it becomes increasingly difficult for us to recover a visionary light upon being. Single-issue activists call us to take sides; but the issue that seems single today dissolves into yet another issue tomorrow. Today the Homeless; yesterday Feminism. Tomorrow, what? The confusion underlines the absence of both a metaphysical or a visionary perspective upon being, so that the *ad hoc* is seemingly the only position allowed in the amorphous contentions within the social and political arena. Willful obstacles to grace prevent spiritual vision. Arrogant assumptions of the *ratio*'s absolutist position prevent a recovery of metaphysical vision.

Through such confusions, the individual is seen as suitably, even heroically, in revolt against any reigning lords of order; individual rights are elevated over both general and absolute good. The concern occurs moment to moment, and the individual justified on the instant in claiming himself free agent. (Look at the clogged judicial calendars, both civil and criminal.) Our political history, given such reflections, will make us see the youth "radical" of the 1960s and the Fundamentalist "radical" of the 1980s as less aberration from a glacial radicalism out of the seventeenth century than as an inevitable spectacle of political and social struggles in the gnostic arena, surfacing from that glacial movement. What is conspicuous, then, is that a term like *individual* becomes raised to a collective symbol, severed by abstraction from the complexity of *person* and thus prevented anchor in the reality of a person's membership in community. We arrive at the new Everyman, whose promised end is a millennial Eden of one sort or another, depending upon the rainbow colors the manipulator of the shibboleth *individual* uses to distract the person from ends proper to person. In this manner, power may be accumulated, persons lured into collective force out of personhood— whether the compass orienting the migration be labeled political North or South, Irreligious Left or Religious Right. Such is the strategy toward occupying or holding centers of power. And a center is held, not at the level of ceremony, but at the level of mechanism, which is why television as mechanics of psychology is so pervasive of the gnostic battles for power. A recognition latent in the popular mind that it is being abused has resulted in the pejorative tone commonly used in saying the word *Washington.* That same suspicion increasingly attaches to *television* and *newspapers,* a sign of hope no doubt.

From what we have so far said, we may be better inclined to recognize structural, mechanistic similarities between contending factions in the political, social, and academic realms. We have systems of ceremony without the sacrament of ceremony; we have manners as a mere convenience. We find closer identity between the Fundamentalist forces and the Secular Humanistic forces than at first supposed. Both operate within the arena prescribed by democratic ideas grown out of post-Renaissance political thought; both subscribe to the rules of that arena. The arena becomes more jungle than clearing, however, when the term *democratic* is obfuscated into *egalitarian,* a manipulation of the arena's typography necessary to the reduction of *person* and of the discrete implications of person into an emptied integer, *individual.* The term *democratic* carries its burden of *egalitarian* to the advantage of any contestant in the struggle for collective power within the naïvely accepted arena. That both contenders in our illustration, the Fundamentalist and the Secular Humanist, are gnostic is suggested by the defense either makes of its current position, through an appeal to the letter of the law in regard to "individual rights" in community. Through a concept of order established by nature abstracted (the letter created out of the body of reality, as Eve from Adam's body—a Nominalist maneuver), the contender nevertheless appeals to a residual sense in us of a commitment to community, a pull toward a fullness of community. That innate inclination, when distorted by an obedience to the letter, prescribes the member from the body of community, thus reducing community at last to mechanism, as person is reduced to individual. One has bones without flesh, let alone any spiritual life that must be breathed into bones and flesh. Reality, fortunately, always runs counter to such reduction. The body may be made to exhale, but it is not easy for it to resist inhaling. And when the body—community or member of community—is stifled, it fights for air, even though it may fight wildly as a drowning man fights. Thus a person becomes aware of the reduction of his nature when he is declared an individual and treated as merely such. Much of our social and political unrest is a consequence of that disquiet, even though the actual causes of unrest are not clearly articulated by the person struggling to regain differentiation, to reclaim the reality of personhood. The point may be put in a shocking way as perceived by disoriented sensibilities: When hierarchy is denied, reality is thus itself denied, leading in the end to our elevating power over love. But one struggles for the higher, even when one struggles blindly. Though one struggle for literal air, in the issue he discovers he struggles for that breath of life in which are resonances beyond the reductionist's sense of life as merely biological.

Forced to affirm the dominance of the letter, one side asserts the letter as prescribed by the formulations of science, the other the letter as prescribed by inherited formulations of Scripture. And so gnostic literalists are embroiled in a chaos, each in the *name* of order asserted to be based on reality. On either hand the principle which is used to justify revolt or opposition to revolt is the gnostic idea divorced of any metaphysical grounds for idea. But without metaphysics, a vision of the complexity of existence is lost. And the most conspicuous of these ideas to our immediate theme of community, leading to present chaos, is the social contract theory. At this late date the individual, discovering inadequacy in his social role insofar as his self-interest is concerned, voids his contract in one way or another. This has been the process of disintegration of community for over two hundred years, to be observed both East and West, but in Western democracies no less than in Eastern Marxism. And in the West, it is no less evident among those acting in the name of the spiritual than among avowed secularists. It becomes too easy, for instance, for any moment's radicals to justify anarchic Happenings, such as the recent bombings of abortion clinics. The analogy here is to the radical Happenings of the 1960s such as *O! Calcutta*. Lest I be misunderstood, I am firmly opposed to abortion. But one's opposition must be built on firmer ground than those shifting sands of social contract.

Since the social contract theory itself depends from exactly the lone principle of advantage to the individual, the sins of the fathers (Locke's, Hobbes's, Rousseau's) will repeatedly set the current fathers' teeth on edge as they attempt to deal with their children who would secede from the inherited contract. The secession is made in the name of tradition, since social contract theory is now most ancient, even given our rather limited sense of history. The current Establishment is caught in a pattern of repetition of error. It is a pattern determined when love is replaced by power, the question then becoming: Which side in the struggle can marshal the greater power—the present Establishment or its seceding members? In this respect, we are experiencing a very real civil war, the final outcome of which is in doubt.

What is distressing about this war is the loss of a ground in valid principle, principle grown out of the nature of reality. In our present terms, what is missing is an understanding of the relation of *eros* and *agape*. In consequence, the warring parties can but succumb again and again to an inordinate love. Through inordinate love the Gnostic dreams a restructuring of creation in his own emptied image: the individual as autonomous. If the young in the 1960s were opened to another species of inordinate love of the world—that love which Dante has dramatized in his Hell in the circles of lust, gluttony, and prodigality—what wonder that having grown older they are discovered to have become stolidly materialistic. A lamenting chorus grows, raised by nostalgic advocates: The "idealistic" fire of the 1960s now only smolders; yesterday's young have "joined the Establishment" in the interest of wealth and worldly comfort. But avarice and sloth are logical extensions out of that initiating confusion of spirit, out of that inordinate love of the sensual, as Dante shows on the descending circles to the inferno's center.

On the other hand, the 1960s Establishment opens to the reaches of Dante's lower Hell, given Dante's scheme of sins—to that perverted love of the self that more subtly feeds on the desire for power than does an excessive love of the world. Anger, envy, pride: Those are the sins out of intellectual subtleties, out of a sophistry that is usually more evident to the child observing his parent than to the parent. (As one goes deeper in Dante's Hell, one meets older and older damned creatures, arriving at last at that most ancient one, Lucifer.) So the civil war, of which we are all now veterans and bear wounds in some degree, has unrecognized metaphysical grounds. That is, though the veteran himself lack a recognition of reality, he is part of that reality and reflects in himself a being commensurate to his actions, whether this be understood by him or not. Not to discover the metaphysical grounds of being is to avoid valid principles of action in the world. And the point here, once more, is that the individual in his relation to community has lost an understanding of *eros* and *agape* in their proper relation to an ordered self and an ordered community. *Eros* without *agape* must result in an inordinate love of the world. But *agape* without *eros* cannot be *agape:* It can only be a banner mislabeled love, under which Gnostic pride pursues power over being.

And that is why Locke's reduction of the family to the level of nature, as nature is understood by gnostic thought, has borne such bitter fruit in our day. In the sacrament of marriage, *eros* and *agape* are joined—*eros* taken up and transformed ordinately into *agape;* the person so loving is oriented beyond the self and so toward a sense of community transcendent of any "social contract" based on self-interest. We suggested that baptism is itself an enlargement of marriage. In the sacrament of baptism, that community of one (a multiplying of husband and wife into community) is the more mysteriously raised. If we say that community is now three—husband, wife, infant—arithmetic continues inadequate. One must see mystically beyond Ptolemaic visions. How inescapably are *three* now *one*—father and mother now a real presence in the infant itself. And in the sacrament of baptism, the infant joins a larger community and carries with him both mother and father, as they have separately carried their own parents into that community. What this means is that the family is a continuing center of community in a most sacramental way. For the family is always both in and beyond the world. So understood, the family becomes crucial to the life of the social body—that is, to the body of community in history. We begin to see that, though important to the necessities of articulating the meaning of society, people in communion *at* this time and *in* this place are not so simply *of* this time and this place, as social determinism would have it. What meditation begins to reveal to us is that in the discrete family (father, mother, child), seen in this explicit place (wherever on Earth), lies all mankind in a manner beyond the limitations of time and space, beyond empirical demonstration. In the family are joined Heaven and Earth, sacramentally. That is, the sacramental seal upon marriage paradoxically unseals the body of family in an openness toward creation. Most important to a present point, the family is opened to its proper membership in the body social. Hence the disintegration of the family as a sacral body must inevitably result in the disintegration of society, as has come to pass. Our restoration of family depends on a recovery of the complexity of love from captivity by power in the post-Renaissance world. Otherwise, there is little hope of a restoration of vitality in the body social. The recovery of love from the obsessions of power cannot be programmed by any establishment, since the recovery is a spiritual one and not a mechanistic one. Neither law nor science will serve as sufficient to the recovery. And that is why the elaborate and loud concerns from within the present power structures of government or sociology or biology over the future of the family must be most cautiously examined. Love is the Church's province, not the government's nor the hard and soft sciences', however much each and all may assist in the recovery. The recognition of the priority of concern for the spiritual dimension of the problem would reduce the divisiveness in society that results from our attempts to solve such local issues as sex education, abortion, and the like.

Out of that joining called marriage, then, comes into existence that most sacred of bodies in nature, the family—second only in sacredness to the inclusive joining of person as member within the body of Christ, within the Church. That is why the social community decays rapidly as soon as marriage is reduced from its sacramental nature. The idea of marriage has been progressively established as a convenience in the ordering of human nature to the advantage of polity, its sacramental dimension largely abandoned. It is imperative, then, that we come to "see" more clearly. We must rediscover that, from the body of the discrete person, with its several memberships, to the body of families in polity, there is revealed a hierarchy—a structure of corporate body peculiar to mankind in that, through right-ordered will, the particular body is brought into configuration out of several memberships. This community is peculiar to man in nature, differing from other divisions of the hierarchic structures in nature. For man participates in the potential body of that natural hierarchic structure through his spiritual nature and by his willing affirmations of complex existence.

If a family becomes a body when two are sacramentally joined, it is clear from what we have said that family is crucial to the corporate being of the separate person on the one hand and to the corporate being of the largely social body on the other. The discrete family—these persons joined at this time and in this place—reaches into time future and place uncertain; it includes not only immediate children, but children's children—to doomsday. In recognizing this opening of the self and of the family upon time, we begin to understand as well an openness of the past into the present, discovering thereby an added dimension to the body of this discrete family, in its living members. The presence so discovered is more than the shadow of history, a hand of a dead past and of a future yet to be conceived. There is a realness in the potential of offspring, in the contingency of family in relation to the future; there is as well a realness in the actuality of predecessors, those presences in time past, bonded to us by the very fact of our discrete existence in this present moment.

It is this larger structure of the family that has been deliberately deconstructed in the period commonly referred to as the modernist, a period (we repeat) including the Renaissance and post-Renaissance sweep of history. That we recognize its deconstruction is necessary to a restoration of community health in our several memberships in community: in that community called the discrete, particular person; in that community called the family;

in that community of the political body ranging from small town or precinct to nation. Recovering viable community is the commanding labor wherever two or three are gathered together. What is important to the members so gathered to recover the ground of community is a clear understanding of the labor in membership. For the member must understand, first of all, the actual gift of discrete self so that an ordinate concert of membership within the self through those gifts may develop. Thus one comes to recognize community as hierarchic structure, communities within communities.

At the most central point of entry into communal structure is the discrete person, in whom all history centers. That is to say, in the discrete person lies the point of intersection of past and future; here one finds the impositions of contingency upon the special gifts of personhood that relate to the vitality of membership in the community of family and community of families. One finds in himself, at this intersection of history with his gifts, his true "calling." And that is why it falls to the individual member to anchor family in the transcendent through nature, even as he becomes discrete member in that body whose head is Christ. (We have already remarked the implicit transformation of earthly family in the sacrament of baptism and marriage.) With that *common* recognition, persons discover the manifestations of *community*. Which is to say, a person discovers the complementary relationships between his discrete gifts and those of others within that living contingency we call creation. And this is to say that community thus emerges as a presence in creation, through which presence mankind's stewardship in creation may be ordinately exercised.

An understanding of community as hierarchic structure requires a very basic consent, at the level of the discrete person—the member—without which consent persons are prevented membership in the fullness of being, in both the integral being of personhood and in the community of family and families. The consent: a willed YES to existence. The consent is first of all an openness to existence, out of the discrete person, a sacramental action of affirmation—of love for existence. It is an affirmation publicly enacted in the sacral marriage vows; at an outer reach of the social community, it is in that consent to the body social spoken of in loose and confused language and emblems under the rubric of patriotism. It is, at its ultimate, a consent to that community to which St. Paul exhorts us, to be expressed in the consenting action of love one of another, that love here and now which is an earnest of our love of God.

When we look at the initiating level of consent, that of the discrete person's affirmation of the existence of the created universe, we need to remember that the consent must be predicated on a prior consent to his own existence. And that prior action is a consent to his existence in all its particularities, not only to his gifts but to the limits of those gifts as well. That consent is a joyful acceptance of finiteness, without which an ordinate relation to the complexity of all creation becomes impossible. For his enlarged consent, moving him toward a community with being, follows only from a proper love of, acceptance of, affirmation of, the self in its finiteness.

At a second level of consent, following the initiating affirmation of one's own particular existence, lies the acceptance of existences other than one's finite self. It is through such consent that an ordinate love of existence enlarges out of the ordinate love of the self. The wellspring of an ordinate love of existence is affirmed in the commandment to love our neighbor as we love ourselves. But in loving myself I go astray if I love my *self* because it is *my* self. That my self *is*—that is the spring of love in creation, in that we are thus already turning from the self as a center outward toward the Cause of that self and of all creation. For ordinate love is possible when desire graced finds its proper ends. The proper end of love cannot be an inversion, a turning upon the self as ultimate center. The ordinate ends of love are the self and the world and God, in a rising complex of desire. This we may glimpse through rational examination and reflection, as distinguished from our act of love. That is, love *thought* or *thought about* and love *lived* are not the same. Even so, because of the gift of the self whose nature is rational being, we must work toward "lived" love through intellect as we may. Put another way, the *ratio* works toward the delicate restoration of loved parts to the Whole of Love. And in this action toward restoration, out of recognitions through intellect, the self becomes not only the more fully its self; it becomes member in a body of selves, in the body of creation, and oriented toward the Cause of creation. In the self's labor of restoration, Adam's bequest, the self discovers itself restored.

The argument as we have made it appears programmatic, as arguments tend to be, for which reason it is important to make a corrective observation. In naming the relationships involved in the actions of love—moving from a proper self-love to a love of family to a love of community, to a fuller love of God—we are not suggesting a formal program, insofar as one might be concerned with a pattern of our becoming abstracted from the experience of our continuing being (our movement, seemingly in time, from consciousness to self-consciousness to a response of the self to the Other). For our strong sense of the history of the self—a present memory—tempts confusion in that country of love which is independent of time, although we discover that country in time. In the realities of love's actions on the soul's way, love's movements seem most variable within narrative patterns of time. At one point, for instance, one may embrace the large community, rejecting both self and family. Or one may cling to family in an imitation of embrace. Movements of love short of a fullness of love are partial, erratic, confusing, even divisive. But so long as the tendency is toward the end of a love enlarging the self, there is a tendency to enlargement beyond the self. The consequent end of enlargements is the fulfillment of the self. Thus the commandment to love our neighbor as ourself is no static commandment; nor is it a program of analytic procedures. It is the governing necessity of our being, requiring action toward being so long as we are in the world, so long as we are on the way. The commandment is at once a direction to an end and a measure of our particular being as we are on our way to an end. It is a law more constant than any law of nature: At every moment of my journey toward full membership in being, that law measures most accurately the acceptable degree of my self-love. The effect of ordinate self-love upon the self, then, is a mysterious transformation, like the metamorphosis of larva into butterfly. But the transformation is slowed or lost by one's attention to it in itself. Pure love is unself-reflecting. Angels do not contemplate their navels. And neither may saints.

To conclude our aside, let us consider for a moment our confusion about self-love that erodes not only the self but community, a confusion which depends upon time as the ultimate justification of the self's existence. Not *all* time, but this moment of my self. As with any human confusion, we may not claim it privately as our own—as belonging to this present moment of history and to myself alone. It is that error of submission to bullying time whereby any present moment is seized by will in a rejection of time. It is an action usually involving a rejection of all else as well. That is why the inclination has given rise to a continuing tradition in our literature, a theme of most poignant effect. It is in the Greeks and Romans and Renaissance poets. It is in us as well. "Had we but world enough and time," it says. And another poet on the point:

> The melody of Eden lost
> Is first and last our gnawing want;
> First lines in old anthologies
> Translate always to *ubi sunt*.

But what is present in those old sayings that seems lost to us is the conditional recognition. *If* there were world enough and time enough, but there isn't. We in our world to the contrary tend to conclude ours a sufficient world, time only left to conquer through technology. The world enough would thereby be transformed to timeless Eden.

I have put the matter thus starkly to emphasize a difference between old arguments for seizing time and our own: The conditional is in the old arguments, an acknowledgment of having lost the timeless so that time must be desperately seized. Our world, having lost the resonance given by memory, lacks even poignancy, though it has ample room for irony if one reflect upon it from a point of detachment from which to view the old world in relation to our own: The older mind is aware of its fallenness; the current mind is fallen but unaware of it. In truth, the fallenness has to do with the loss of a timeless world, the country of love to which there is suitable passport always available through self-love, that first application necessary. The soul's true country is lost, except insofar as there continues a hunger for it in the soul even when the soul is almost oblivious to the calling. The valid hunger itself exacerbates the erosion of self, of soul. And an evidence of this self-denigration is our ravenous seizing of the present moment, but under the auspices of implacable time and not of love.

We must here insist on an appropriate self-love, which is ours from any point at which we may recognize the self as existing. But self-love, confused by willful intellect, becomes perverted self-love. The soul becomes no longer steward of the world and time, but their slave. And when there is a concert of souls so enslaved, poignant lament such as Horace's or Herrick's or Marvell's transmutes to deconstruction of being, a programming of time and the world by the programmed soul, which has little time for music, poignant or otherwise. Why lament is necessary, we see in the actual words of a university president: "We must find a way to reprogram nature." One has in these words, not the tensions of self-love in an aging youth but a condition of the soul properly suiting it to Dante's *Inferno*. And because that condition exists for us as pervasive of our social being, the collapse of self-love, rather than its burgeoning ordinately in community, is everywhere symptomatic in our decayed community.

Such summary conclusion needs support, not a support out of statistical survey, but from a focusing of the self's awareness upon its present condition in community. Let us look together. Lately we have been made aware of the fierce resistance of the fetus in its mother's womb to its own extinction by saline solution. A film showing a fetus's desperate struggle against death is widely circulated, the disturbing quality in the event perhaps recovering for us that ground out of which the tensions of self-love are once more made poignant. Had it but a little more of the world, a little more of time, the struggle the fetus makes in its wild desperation might take on a form whereby we might better recognize the heroic in it. Nevertheless, we have in the filmed event an undeniable evidence of the self-love I wish to characterize as an initiating of the self into the complexities of being, being which is pointed to by the world and time. For the old temptation to seize more than world enough and the old shadow of slow-chapped time indeed point to a center to which world and time are only peripheral: They underline being itself. This death of a fetus, dramatized out of current history to us by film, represents a literal event at as far a remove from *self-conscious* awareness of death's threat to the being of the self as we may imagine in man.

Provided only that the fetus survive in a developing self-awareness, that creature may be said to emerge potentially into a higher order of love that binds the hierarchy of its own developing being, its discrete but not autonomous actuality. Self-love unifies that hierarchy of the soul in its blossoming, from its biological dimension through all manifestations of the soul's complexity. (For the biological is not separate from the fullness meant by the term *soul,* though our world attempts to make a separation.) Within that unique personhood here described, this sovereign being, the soul, must deal intellectually with the question of its own being; it must affirm its existence or deny and reject that existence. It must imitate that action of absolute being of which it is image, that being whose symbol for us is YAHWEH, I AM THAT I AM. It must say, "I am." Or it will say in a variety of ways, "I am not." And it must do so intellectually, since the special differentiation of the human soul is its rational intellect.

Let us note, then, the fetus' desperate struggle to survive when other souls, through intellectual powers brought upon that fetus by other (adult?) souls' actions of "I am Not," would obliterate it. This confrontation, reduced to the trivial by science's reductionism of being, is from our perspective indeed heroic. The fetus demonstrates by action of being an ancient intellectual recognition about being. Homer gives it poignant drama as Odysseus, at the border of Hades, greets his old warrior companion Achilles. Odysseus praises the shade of Achilles, with a stirring of envy, as the great hero celebrated throughout the world of light. Achilles is remembered among both gods and living men. But the shade of Achilles rejects such shadowy eminence as memory, that false life within the memory of living men. He would, he says, rather be under the sun as slave to a landless man—the most desperate condition of life in that ancient heroic world—than king of all the dead. Later in our literature, in a compromise with the world and time, Aeschylus has an old man of his chorus assert against Cassandra's fatalism, "He who dies last in some sort dies best." Since these ancient literary recognitions of the gift of life, whatever its circumstances, philosophers and then theologians have ever contended with this one theme binding humanity. But what we call attention to here is a most elemental affirmation of life, not by poet or philosopher or theologian, but by the unknown fetus struggling against its destruction. By its action it shows us an affirmation of self-love, an affirmation of the gift of life itself.

Ours is no such heroic age as Homer's, though there are heroes. It is rather a grab and throwaway one, in which neither shade out of history nor soul in a presence is much remembered in relation to the mystery of being. In our world one may scrap life or buy it on whim, abortion and surrogate parentage alike reducing human existence to the simply biological, ignoring even current knowledge, secular though it is, of that dimension of the biological elevated to the science of psychology. The intellectual climate within which we live is that of science's reductionism. That reductionism of being to the merely material, rising only to the level of the biological, provides the popular mind with an authority it hungers for, one it may accept on faith through what that same authority increasingly justifies as the individual's most valued response to existence, its feeling.

This fundamentalism of feeling, accepted by the layman's faith in the gnostic priesthood of science, finds a release that passes as salvation in the moment's whim. In respect to this perverse address to the mystery of the gift of life, made spectacular through abortion and surrogate motherhood, the operative whim is the convenience or inconvenience to the whimsical individual as it encounters another discrete soul, the fetus. This principle of whim of course is unsupportable by any logical appeal beyond the moment's convenience. For if the moment's whim is the governing principle, it makes no difference whether the absent or intruding soul is fetus, infant, child, or aging parent. If the fullness of being has its limit established by the power of those beings who are fortunately arrived already at the level of power in nature, it is of no consequence within that view of being whether the particular instance of the separate soul is fetus or three-year-old or eighty-year-old. It becomes as consistent within the view of life here operative to wait till the bought creature is three years old or five years old, so that the levels of technocracy now available can measure its biological defects to decide whether to keep or cast out the bought creature. The point applies whether the bought soul is to be implanted in or discarded from the womb. That the principle put thus starkly is still disturbing may be cause for some hope. That the principle is already operative in the quasi-legal contracts involving surrogate motherhood is clear: The purchasing "father" sometimes makes as a condition of his purchase the right to abort the fetus if technology shows prospects of defect in it.

In relation to the dominant faith we hold in life as simply biological, only the memory of genes is considered holy, since the
consequential in biological life is believed to rest fully in the mystery of genes. But even that memory is held holy only insofar as
the cult's priests perform biological miracles—that is, manipulate
being within the arena of time. It is thus "feasible" to value gene
memory, but it is primitive and retrograde to hold on to other species of memory. In this brave new world a-making, this world
of made-to-order or throwaway life, we hardly earn that disturbed puzzlement growing among us over the rising suicide rate
among teenagers. When we see the circumstances from a position removed from the reductionist climate in which we live and
breathe and have what limited being is allowed us, we might well
conclude that the concern for teen suicide within that climate of
thought is rather more closely akin to our similar growing alarms
(reported on the same evening news) over the threat to our comfort from the mountains of garbage we produce. The enormous
bulk of that garbage would seem to make throwaway commodi-
ties increasingly less convenient, given the common principle
within the reductionist climate: an impiety toward being itself.
Indeed, there may be in the offing a common abstract address to
the problem of garbage disposal for New York City and London
and Tokyo and to the problem of the population explosion itself.
We shall rather certainly move in that direction, I believe, if we
do not recover a sense of a necessary piety toward being which
makes us look more closely and deeply at the order of being beyond the whim of the moment, whether the whim be individual
or collective.

Our concern for being is governed by the moment's whim.
But that a fetus or an infant should be bought and sold through
whim requires a more careful description of the term *whim*.
Otherwise we shall be left with whim as an aspect of biological
being, a glow of the moment out of biological complexity convenient to the organism and therefore biologically justified, so long
as that organism or a collective of such organisms are in a position to exercise power over other organisms. What we are dealing
with in *whim* as here used is in its true name *perverted love;* it is
that inordinate self-love which a few scattered memories still
hold as the most heinous sin of which the soul is capable. That

scattered remnant are enabled by that memory to stand aside from the reductionist climate of the modern world to see the deeper implication of governing whims. When we accept the commerce in fetuses as reasonable and desirable for the moment's satisfaction to the particular customer of being who wields power over the fetus, we should not be surprised by an ultimate perversion of communal love by those who have for a moment escaped that constricting power—those at a turning point where they must either join in consent to the general reductionist faith, the secular fundamentalism, or must find some way to reject that dubious citizenship. The dilemma of some teenagers lies precisely in their recognizing the necessity of an action already advanced in our argument, the necessity of saying yes to being or no to being.

Our young are faced with saying yes to a being reduced to the level of technological science; it should not be surprising, then, that we have the current problem of teen suicide. One dimension of it, I suggest, is analogous to the action of the fetus against the intruding saline solution, though to see the analogy requires our seeing as well how life may appear to the disoriented teenager. If life is merely an existence at the biological level, the conscious recognition of that circumstance means already that the soul which recognizes it is at some remove from the circumstance. The absence of a prospect for the full promise of being that is within the gift of being itself, within the soul, is the most blatant aspect of the reduced world of being confronting the teenager. There is no reason we should suppose it a rational understanding at all. In fact, it is quite the contrary, for the manipulations and reductions of the rational faculty by the post-Renaissance world are such that the teenager hardly has the use of the rational faculty. If one need evidence to the point, he may look at the gross level of our current concerns over the failures in our educational systems.

The initiating movement toward suicide in a teenager is that of the *intellectus,* in which respect we may at last see the analogy between some suicides and the fetus struggling for being. For the act of suicide may itself be just such a struggle. It may be, paradoxically, a confused attempt to say no to a world in which being is first negated and then negation itself raised in an idolatry, in a religion oriented to the darker gods. That is the religion of secular gnosticism. The argument here is by no means an approval of suicide by the confused teenager; it is rather an attempt to understand how such a soul might come to this ultimate perversion of love, suicide. Indeed, suicide is the inevitable symptom one ought to expect out of the general spiritual malady that passes for biological and psychological health in our world. And my contention is that the root cause of the disease in our being is the willed disorientation of the self from the holiness of being. Our young, even when nurtured as fetus and infant on mother's milk of being, as they come to the formative years of the *ratio* breathe within a reduced intellectual climate, that of the modernist world's contaminated air.

Now *all* teenagers do not commit suicide, as all teenagers do not submit to reduction within the reductionist world even though they yet must breathe its climate. But the intellectual climate does provide a condition suited to confusions of the *intellectus* through failures of the *ratio*. Struggling against the sterilization of both *ratio* and *intellectus,* as the fetus struggles against the contaminants in the life-giving fluids of the uterus, the confused soul might well come to Socrates' position on life. It may do so if the only world it sees is reduced from the full measure of a life it hungers for. Death, Socrates argues, is necessarily good. For at death either the soul is released from the evils of the body and its surroundings—the shadows of being rather than being itself—and may come to fulfilled being. Or the soul, along with the shadow body, ceases altogether in an absolute nonbeing. Either, Socrates says, is preferable to the state of so-called life in the so-called world. (We have already recalled Achilles' response to this argument.) Some of our young, I am suggesting, have come to the same conclusion, not through Socratic thought, but out of a whimsical response to the chilling climate of death that is inescapable in our grab and throwaway world. Some, out of confused self-love, commit suicide on whim.

We raise this question of a general confusion about love, starkly illustrated by teen suicide, in the interest of our central concern, namely, a concern for some prospect of recovering a rightly ordered love of being through the intellectual gifts that persist beyond all our biological reductionisms of life. When one has reached a level of being whereby there is an undeniable experience by the self of itself, a level of knowing beyond the desperate affirmation of being by fetus or the infant struggling for survival, the knowing self is aware as well of its separateness from the Other. Where the fetus-infant sort of knowing is out of an incipient *intellectus*, this new knowing is at the threshold of the *ratio*'s participation in the soul's being. But if the self cease to love itself, it will not love any other. Its condition is that of spiritual despair. Unless its knowing reveals through an opening love of the self that largeness of the country of love, a country beyond the moment of time to which it is tempted to respond through whim, it must perish. And in such confused mind biological suicide is grasped as the ready means to obliterating all knowing. Or so it may appear to the despairing soul.

It will not follow from such advanced knowing, from this arrival on the threshold of the *ratio*'s participation in the discrete soul's being, that the soul will therefore engage in an orderly, sequential or "rational" unfolding of love whereby the soul attempts to recover that lost country of love which is always present to it, even when it finds itself breathing the distorted climate of being within the modernist world it inhabits. It is nevertheless through those intellectual faculties in concert, the *ratio* and the *intellectus*, that the incipient lover (the soul) may turn the more fully toward being and in turn be enfolded in the larger orders of being such as family and community and Church. For one of the conditions of the fallen soul's existence in time is that it struggle to recover its orientation to some loved Other. And from the fetus' struggle to exist to the child's to the teenager's to the old and wise Socrates' struggle, the necessities of coming-to-be are insistent. At the spiritual level of this insistent struggle to be, one sees a common dimension to the discrete soul, then, whether one look at the fetus or troubled teenager or ancient. It is the dimension of personhood, the flowing coming-to-be which only through the limitations of the finite rational mind is arrested in moments such as those designated *fetus* or *teenager* or *old man or woman*.

We are suggesting that though when we arrest the flow of the discrete soul's becoming to such designations there may appear a patterned enlargement, we are looking at such pattern under the auspices of the *ratio*. Neither philosopher nor theologian, and certainly not social planner, may establish an inevitable working pattern in the events of the soul's becoming so that any soul may by a pattern be rescued. We discover tendencies suggestive of patterns of becoming, and we may properly use them, with discrete piety toward those patterns—so long as we remember that we engage a creature whose true country is that of love, a country in the orders of being to which we have access in limited ways, since our powers are finite. We may suppose a pattern the more discernible perhaps at the summary end of its journeying, at the end of its being-on-the-way. More properly, the soul may itself discern such a seeming pattern in its own being, which is why the witness of the wise to his own being bears more authority than our rational appropriation of such witness to our attempted programs of soul-making in general. From its summary end, at a point of transition out of finite being, the soul may see its history as a map made within the seeming wilderness of nature and history. At the setting forth, the world of self and of other must seem largely undifferentiated wilderness, points to which our finite science, our finite knowing, may properly speak. Properly, so long as governed by a recognition of the finitude of such science. That is, properly, so long as spoken with that piety due the mystery of being. So long as we begin to recognize that our true country transcends our weak patterns.

In the light of this self-reminder, I emphasize here that once the soul is awakened to the mystery of its own existence and to the mystery of the complexity of the life of itself and of the other, the soul may discover through the offices of *ratio* and *intellectus* that its growth is neither simply random nor accidental. It may well come to practice, through right will, an orderly, and even a patterned, recovery of ways to the fulfillment of its gifts, a practice through the differentiating gift to the created soul for its being-on-the-way: the guiding offices of the *ratio* and *intellectus*. This we affirm out of witness borne by the wise through the guiding offices of *ratio* and *intellectus*. The disciplines of virtuous being, given our fallen nature, would seem to require an active movement toward recovery under the auspices of mind. The orderliness of this endeavor of mind may well appear programmatic, but it does so at the level of spectacle. We need only remember, in our concern for proper piety, that spectacle is the sign of the action of being and not the action itself. The true country of action is that of love, upon whose borders we sojourn in our becoming, through the gift of our finitudes.

If our approach to the existence of community is sound, it will help us understand why community is so confused and fragmented in our time, why community seems so little a body. We look at the increasingly fragmenting body, at the entropy of alienation, and find the dissolution an effect of inordinate self-love. The family, taken as discrete community, shows the shock of self-love forced upon its body from within by its discrete members; family shows more spectacularly the destructions made by an external social policy long since devoid of community understanding and given over to the mechanics of manipulation through abstractions. What is missing is a common consent to the being of the several body of community: person, family, social entity. What we discover is that when we no longer work outward from the central membership in the self and of the self, we doom any larger community as well. At the level of policy, we are reduced to *ad hoc* attempts at order. *Ad hoc* attempts to establish an ordered polity are the inevitable desperate attempts when the separation of particular member from community has occurred. Meanwhile, the particular member exercises his attempt at order out of no metaphysical sense of community. With varying degrees of authority, depending upon the intellectual strength of the individual and upon the power at his disposal, a particular "solution" may dominate and may continue dominant in the political and social arena over considerable time. For *ad hoc* attempts are not actions at *a* moment, but more properly actions lacking established principle. *Ad hoc* community structures have dominated our history for centuries now. Since the Renaissance, we live increasingly within the tradition of the *ad hoc*. This primitivism of intellect we come to praise as sophistication. But given the rational gift of our being, we must rediscover that only a metaphysical ground will rescue community from the alternative of recurring *ad hoc* response to the complexity of existence. Meanwhile, with deliberate intent and over a period of time, we continue to jettison the metaphysical grounding of the person and of community that we may float free of what we have come to believe an inhibiting and enslaving reality, the reality of being itself.

Such deconstructions of our own being, lacking sound meta-physical principles, have inevitably become actions against existence. The loss has been that love proper to the self and to community.

Such has been the program of modern gnosticism. In a pursuit of power it has preached as doctrine and as principle of significant action the advantage to the self, though disguised in shibboleths like *society* or *humanity* or even *family*. The end is a control of collective selves whose common action is said to be based on self-interest. That has been the direction taken by social contract philosophies, evinced in Marxism on the one hand and Libertarianism on the other. It has meant a reduction of membership to a collective on the one hand and to a separation and elevation of member to an absolute entity on the other; leading from mankind seen as mechanistic machine on the one hand to mankind seen as anarchic sovereignties, the extreme limit of plurality called individualism, on the other. (The suggestion here is of parameters; the gradations within extremes are infinite.)

The desire for identity, so intimately involved in our rage for "liberty," is most difficult to order in relation to a proper self-love, since that desire when dislocated even slightly from its proper end makes it all but impossible to accept the limits of the being of the self. In this dislocation, terms like *individual* and *individuality* usurp the idea of *person* and *personhood*. *Personality* in its popular sense becomes an obsession, symptomatic of the dislocation. When one accepts his own particular existence and existences other than that of the self within the limits of finitude, a delicately, nicely balanced love becomes possible, the pious consent to existence which we would affirm as central to a fullness of being. The dislocation of that proportionate love may lead to an unacceptable sacrifice of the self to the other, a violation of self-love; the self is thus denigrated in a passive obliteration of the self. One's discrete membership in the body of creation becomes distorted. It is not easy to illustrate this condition. I have suggested as an instance in fiction William Faulkner's Ike McCaslin in *Go Down, Moses*. (See my "Separation of Grace from Nature," *Why Flannery O'Connor Stayed Home*.) A difference I wish to point out is that between surrendering one's own existence in an oblivion of the self, as Ike does in rejecting actions of stewardship incumbent upon him in consequence of his membership in family, and the giving of the self to existence, which has been so movingly shown us by the life of Mother Teresa. Perhaps the question is one of the degree more than of the essence of self-action, but I think not. It is rather the difference between a Christ-like surrender of the self (as with Mother Teresa) and a surrender in which one confuses himself with Christ in an attempt to expiate not the self but the world (as with Ike's attempt to pay his family debt to existence as if he were the Second and not the First Adam).

However we decide this delicate distinction in the actions of love, the inclination to excess by an Ike McCaslin is a more improbable distortion of true self-love than is a distortion with which we are more familiar. The probable distortion is that whereby one is excessively committed to the self at the expense of the largesse of existence. It is as old a self-destruction as Lucifer's "I will not serve." And here, surely, is the source of contamination of, infection of, that body of community which is epidemic in us. The decay of ordinate self-love exacerbates; the self becomes caught in an accelerated distortion, self-ravishing in its very feeding, as with Dante's she-wolf on the outskirts of Hell. That she-wolf's presence in the several modes of community's address to the world—in economics, science, politics, education—is traceable to the elevation of the self over the body of community. The concept *self* ceases to be a reality and becomes shibboleth for the manipulations of being itself by gnostic power. This manipulation goes under several banners, usually in the name of community or humanity or the like—names that disguise what is truly involved: the self exercising its given powers in self-interest. Good names are given bad causes, till good names themselves become bad. Nor may we rely simply on discovering Machiavellian intent. Sometimes sophistry is more easily recognized by someone other than the sophist. It is a problem not yet easily resolved whether Stalin and Hitler were "insincere" in their professions that their acts intend ultimately a general good, which reminds us that ends and means must be intimately involved through some sound, recognizably transcendent moral ground. Evil's subtle appropriations of "sincerity" involve not only the deliberate lie but the unseeing lie as well—false vision—so that we must remember always that our words may bear false witness not only through intent but out of blindness.

In pursuit of this point, one should read Willmoore Kendall's analysis of the social contract developed by Hobbes, Locke, and Rousseau (see Chapter 5 of his *Conservative Affirmation in America*). The idea of social contract is *ad hoc* in being against, rather than out of, traditional understandings of political community. It establishes a speculative theory, which is not supported by its being measured against experience, as Kendall argues effectively. Positing a state of nature, in something of the same way neo-Darwinians must posit a "soup" of matter as a point of departure, there follows an assertion of compact made among individuals emerging from under the rule of nature, a compact whereby the individual bargains his natural rights for community safety, establishing thereby the "social contract" presumed to order the political sphere. Kendall points out that self-preservation—self-interest—thus becomes the ground of justice in the moral realm of community. Such a contract is binding only so long as the individual party to the contract (as opposed to a member of a body in the old disposition of community) is satisfied. The individual's interests are protected, but *interests* is limited to the self *as defined by the self,* the condition made possible since the self does not surrender irrevocably its natural rights. By such a conditional surrender of natural rights, the separate self buys advantage to the self. Such a contract, then, allows no recourse to authority higher than self-interest, so that force is the ultimate arbiter. What comes to disturb us when we recognize this condition of social contract is that, through what is purported to be thoughtful vision, the principle of anarchy becomes intrinsic to the new version of community. The slow, glacial movement in social polity gradually turns the buried principle to the surface, a principle pervasive of our political history in this century. Anarchy is increasingly accepted as the principle of action by individuals, who justify themselves by a mystical appeal to natural rights. Society, community, is held hostage increasingly *within the formal structures* grown slowly out of social contract theory. If terroristic acts by Muslim fanatics are the more spectacular, they are not more debilitating to community than the legalized anarchy justified by the letter of the law derived from the principles of social contract.

If we look at the Renaissance world, not as is popularly done— as a growth and burgeoning—but as a fragmentation of community, we might discover the history of the post-Renaissance world already written for it by Thucydides. He examines the world of the collapsing Greek city-states and finds self-interest emerging as the highest authority. If we take the Hobbes-Locke-Rousseau world to include our own, what Thucydides says of the Peloponnesian states, in Chapter 10 of his *Peloponnesian War*, seems apt description of ours:

Revolution thus ran its course from city to city, and the places which it arrived at last from having heard what had been done before carried to a still greater excess the refinement of their invention as manifested in the cunning of their enterprises and the atrocity of their reprisals. Words had to change their ordinary meaning and to take that which was not given them. Reckless audacity came to be considered the courage of a loyal ally; prudent hesitation, specious cowardice; moderation was held to be a cloak for unmanly ability to see all sides of a question and inaptness to act on any. . . . To succeed in a plot was to have a shrewd head, to divine a plot a still shrewder; but to try to provide against having to do either was to break up your party and to be afraid of your adversary. In fine, to forestall an intending criminal, or to suggest the idea of a crime where it was wanting, was equally commended, until even blood became a weaker tie than party, from the superior readiness of those united by the latter to dare everything without reserve; for such associations had not in view the blessings derivable from established institutions but were formed by ambition for their overthrow; and the confidence of their members in each other rested less on any religious sanction than upon complicity in crime. . . . Oaths of reconciliation, being only proffered on either side to meet an immediate difficulty, only held good so long as no other weapon was at hand.

From such a decayed society, one of the issues may be tyranny. A likely ground for the growth of various tyrannies is the "social contract."

If, instead of looking at this *ad hoc* political arena, we should begin nearer the point where the ground of the self was lost, we might well begin with Occam and Descartes, and follow the growing loss at least so far as John Stuart Mill's melding of Locke and Descartes in his "On Liberty." We may then see an effect on community emerging from the seductive argument for an "Open Society." And again, Kendall has the illuminating analysis of Mill and the flaws in Mill's argument, Chapter 6 of his *Conservative Affirmation in America*. Kendall concludes of the social contract theory, "Insofar as it is a generally-accepted principle of modern political philosophy and modern politics that the purpose of society, government, and law is to minister to the self-interest of members of society, rather than to the perfection of man's nature or to the attunement of human affairs to the will of God, we again stand in the presence of the influence of the contract philosophers, and can by no means speak of their 'position' as one that subsequent generations have refuted." That the principle of contract is modified by Mill's concept of liberty is sufficiently apparent at the level of politics in such avenues to power as the legalized political action committees (PACs) to support individual congressmen and by the horde of lobbyists at every level of government. What is reflected is the extension of political plurality to the point that each self is a sovereign of the realm, sometimes joining with like-minded sovereignties in a separate social compact to direct political affairs from points of vantage outside the political order. The phenomenon of single-issue political forces is symptom of a collapse of political order out of the "evolutionary" theory of social contract philosophy.

We are dealing here with what I (and others) have characterized as gnostic modes of manipulating existence. Operated more or less deliberately through the *ratio,* the gnostic's persuasive strength lies in the modern myth of the self—the myth of individuality as an absolute, in the light of which there can be no social body, only a gathering of individuals maneuvering for self-preservation. The self as absolute is a principle of gnostic power, whether advanced by the philosopher or theologian or politician—all of which good callings of the self are easily appropriated to serve bad things. Thus the philosopher asserts his own mind the cause of being; or the theologian (if a descendant of the ancient Gnostic) asserts his own soul to be excluded from the dependence implied by the term *creation;* or the politician, in the name of individual rights, molds individuals into power blocks mislabeled community. In every instance, these glacial aberrations melt as they move. The reality of creation—of existence— will inevitably intrude and confound false positions. For in the human realm, actual existence commands an ordinate relation of the self to the other, in a community of being. Meanwhile, such is our fallen nature, we cling desperately to a contradiction worshipped as if it were a religious paradox: infinite individuality. While elevating individuality as the godhead of self, we will to reject the insistent reality that must be accepted: When we move from *that we are* (which is shared with all creation) to *what we are* (which is particular, making us discrete), "individuality" is reduced to finitude, the condition of reality requiring humility. Meanwhile (so the struggle goes on), at the level of the spectacle of personhood, *personality* becomes the focus. (See *People.*) But personality's true ground, we are slowly forced to see, is measured in the fullness of being in the person. That fullness is realized—must be realized—through love, ordinate love. First of the self, out of which grows membership in the body of existence, the communion of love, the community of being.

And so we insist upon a reality, even if the words of that insistence are not themselves a sufficient witness to that reality. The end of our exploring, as Eliot says, is "to arrive where we started / And know the place for the first time." Thus we conclude as we set out: The body of community exists. It is an actual thing which we know or know of, independent of the verbal concept through which we mean to affirm it.

Index

Abortion, 136, 142, 144, 150–51, 152
Academy. *See* Higher education
Achilles, 151, 155
Action: versus spectacle, 32, 34–35, 43–45, 101, 133, 157–58
Advertising, 32–34, 105–106
Aeschines, 69
Aeschylus, 151
Agape, 130–31, 133, 135, 142, 143
Aging. *See* Old age
AIDS virus, 53
Alchemists, 45
Alcibiades, 51
Anarchy, 34, 161
Aquinas, St. Thomas, 7, 8–9, 14, 17–18, 22, 37, 39, 42–43, 64–68, 122
Aristotle, 9, 11, 19, 32, 48, 61, 63, 91, 110
Art: versus science, 54–55, 131. *See also* Liberal arts education
Astronomy, 8
Augustine, St., 65

"Back to the Basics," 49, 74, 94, 115–16, 117
Bacon, Francis, 19, 63, 114
Baptism, 143–44, 146
Barbarisms, 97
Barfield, Owen, 9
Baudelaire, Charles, 103
Beauty, 61–62, 65, 89–90
Berlinski, David, 50–53, 57, 62
Biotechnology, 45
Blacks, 27
Body of community, 125–128, 164
Bound/bind, 3–5, 21, 28

Brain hemispheres, 65
Brooks, Cleanth, 96
Bureaucratic establishment, 136
Burke, Edmund, 19, 55

Cartesian gnosticism, 62, 63
Cassandra, 151
Center for Theology and the Natural Sciences, 9
Chaucer, Geoffrey, 15, 55, 73, 104–105
Chemistry, 70
Chesterton, G. K., 104, 107–108, 109
Children. *See* Youth
Children's rights, 57–58
Chomsky, Noam, 52
Church, 126–27, 145
Clichés, 20, 21, 73–75, 76
Colleges and universities. *See* Higher education; Liberal arts education
Committees, 83–84
Communication, 99
Community: and words, 3, 4, 100; nation as, 23; integrity of, 38; of scholars, 47–55; gifts of particularity and, 54–55, 80, 102–103; mystery of, 68, 82–83; and language, 79; Christendom and, 83; compared with committees, 83–84; family and, 84–87, 144–45; past and future and, 87–88 and liberal arts education, 88–95; fragmentation of, 94, 114, 141–142, 158, 161–62; relationship with academy, 100, 101–102; characterizations of, 119–25; rational community, 120; body of community, 125–29, 164;

definition of, 125–26; and persons encountering each other, 129–30; erosion during 1960s and 1970s, 131–35; erosion during 1980s, 134–41; consent and, 146–58; membership in, 146; persons and, 146; *ad hoc* structures of, 158–59
Company, 79
Concepts, 120, 123
Contract theory. *See* Social contract theory
Creation, 163
Critical realism, 9–12

Dance of life, 101, 104, 109
Dante Alighieri, 62, 63, 64, 69, 84, 101, 111, 121–23, 142, 143, 150, 160
Darwinism, 13, 51, 129, 137
Dawson, Christopher, 28
Dedalus, Stephen, 14–15, 16, 52
Democratic, 140
Democritus, 12
Descartes, René, 9, 19, 48, 63, 71, 114, 162
Dialectic, 113
Dictionaries, 4, 6–7, 76
Divine right of kings, 128
Docudrama, 32, 34
Donne, John, 85

Economics, 53
Education: definition of, 4; purpose of, 33, 34, 38, 78–80, 88, 91, 107, 110; grades and, 78–79; length of time needed for, 92; gift of restlessness, 93–95; confusion of morality with, 103; distortions of reality in, 111; and psychological development, 113–14. *See also* Faculty; Higher education; Liberal arts education; Students
Egalitarian, 140
Einstein, Albert, 7, 10, 11, 12, 18, 79, 109
Eliot, T. S., 21–22, 23, 63, 67–68, 69, 101, 109, 164
Elitism, 24–26
Elizabeth I, Queen, 96
Emerson, Ralph Waldo, 16, 19
Empiricism, 62, 128

Eros, 130–31, 133, 135, 142, 143
Establishment, 134, 136, 137–38, 142, 143
Etiquette, 38–40
Evangelical television, 136
Evil, 80, 160
Evolution, 51, 129

Facts, 16–17, 44, 62
Faculty: relationship with students, 6, 38–39; words and, 7; responsibilities of, 37, 45, 47, 78, 80, 90, 91–92; quality and caliber of, 92–93; words used by, 100; difficulties of liberal arts teacher, 114–15. *See also* Education; Higher education; Liberal arts education; Students
False witness, 25, 27, 44, 46
Falstaff, 40–42
Familiarity, 39
Families, 58, 83, 84–87, 128–31, 134–35, 143–46, 158
Faulkner, William, 20, 159
Faust theme, 121
Feminism, 138
Fetus, 150–51, 152, 153, 154, 156
Fools, 56–60, 63, 64
Fourteenth Amendment, 27
Freudianism, 26, 61, 137
Frost, Robert, 67, 78
Fundamentalism: religious, 10, 11, 51, 134–41; scientific, 11–12; intellectual, 51; secular, 154
Fundamentalist movement, 134–41

Geology, 8
Gilson, Étienne, 51, 52
Ginsberg, Allen, 56, 60
Gnosticism: 138–39, 142, 163; Cartesian, 62, 63; secular, 155; modern, 159; ancient, 163
God, 17–18, 20–21, 49–50, 51, 64, 83, 122, 147, 148, 163
Grades, 78
Grammar, 113, 114–15, 116
Greek language, 24–26, 28, 29, 36

Hal, Prince, 40
Hardy, Thomas, 36
Harre, Rom, 49, 50, 65
Harris, Joel Chandler, 96

Hauerwas, Stanley, 57–58
Hawthorne, Nathaniel, 19, 20, 104
Hegel, Georg Wilhelm, 128
Heidegger, Martin, 71
Heraclitus, 60, 65, 67
Herrick, Robert, 150
Higher education: professionalism
    and, 23, 29, 31–32, 45–46, 49;
    criticisms of 31, 33–36, 69–71,
    101–102, 105, 111, 114–18; isola-
    tion and, 33–34; purpose of, 33, 34,
    38, 78–80, 88, 91, 107, 110; intel-
    lectual confusions and, 35–36;
    specialization and, 35–36, 47–48,
    49, 53–54; and virtue, 42–47, 80,
    91–92; spectacle versus action
    in, 43–45; community of scholars,
    47–55; academic integrity, 49–55;
    public relations and, 69–70; temp-
    tations to abandon purpose of, 69;
    and witness to truth, 69; "new
    knowledge" and, 70–73; publish-
    or-perish syndrome, 70–71; grades
    in, 78–79; and importance of
    words, 78–79, 99–100; student re-
    sponsibilities, 78, 80, 91; teacher re-
    sponsibilities, 78, 90, 91–92;
    committees in, 83–84; responsibili-
    ties to family and community, 83;
    quality and caliber of faculty,
    92–93; quality and caliber of un-
    dergraduates, 95–100; abuse of
    language in academic officers,
    98–99; relation of community to,
    100, 101–102; leading universities,
    105. See also Education; Faculty;
    Liberal arts education; Students
Hinduism, 29
Hitler, Adolph, 160
Hobbes, Thomas, 128, 142, 161, 162
    151
Homer, 1–2, 20, 29, 67, 79, 109,
Honor, 41–42
Hope, 42–43
Hopkins, Gerard Manley, 6, 63, 67
Horace, 150
Hotspur, 41–42
Human development, 110–13
Humanities: versus science, 68. See
    also Liberal arts education
Huxley, Aldous, 47
Hymns, 3–5

Ideas, 79–80
Imagery, 76–77
Imagination, 76
Individual/individuality, 102–104,
    138–41, 159, 163–64. See also Per-
    son, personhood
Individual rights, 141, 163
Integrity, 38, 42, 44, 46–47, 49–55,
    64, 103–104. See also Virtue
Intellect, 14, 33–34, 64–69, 110,
    123–24
Intellectual fundamentalism, 51
Intellectus, 67, 68, 79–80, 120–21,
    122, 131, 154–55, 156, 157
Intuition, 67
Ionian physics, 12
Isolation, 33–34, 109

Jackson, Andrew, 27
Jaki, Stanley, 49–50, 51, 52
Jastrow, Robert, 8
Jaynes, Julian, 65, 66
Johnson, Samuel, 7
Jones, David, 97, 107–108
Jonson, Ben, 55
Joyce, James, 14–15, 16, 52
Julian of Norwich, 22

Kant, Immanuel, 19
Keats, John, 19, 43, 63, 64, 66, 67
Kendall, Willmoore, 129, 161, 162–63
Knowledge, 70–74, 122–25. See also
    Truth; Wisdom

Language: growth of, 6; problem
    with, 13–14; definition of, 26; and
    the past, 26; as common property,
    54; mystery of, 75; and community,
    79; abuse of, 97–99. See also Words
Lanier, Sidney, 76–78
Latin language, 24–26, 28, 36
Lear, King, 58
Lewis, C. S., 85–86
Liberal arts education: purpose of, 19,
    91, 114; principles underlying,
    22–23; arguments against, 24–29,
    36; defense of, 24; intellectual con-
    fusions and, 35–36; specialization
    and, 35–36; science versus art,
    54–55; community and, 88–95;
    criticisms of, 101–102; barriers to,
    114–18; remedial grammar and,

116–17. *See also* Education; Faculty; Higher education; Students
Libertarianism, 159
Liberty, 159, 162, 163
Lies, 25. *See also* False witness
Life-style, 108–109
Linguistics, 52
Lobbyists, 163
Locke, John, 19, 128–31, 137, 138, 142, 143, 161, 162
Love, 135, 142, 143, 147–48, 153, 155–58, 164. See also *Agape; Eros*
Lovelace, Richard, 62

Machiavellianism, 160
Manicheans, 12
Manners, 38–40, 130, 140
Maritain, Jacques, 102
Marlowe, Christopher, 121
Marriage, 130–31, 143, 145, 146
Marvell, Andrew, 62, 150
Marxism, 137, 159
Materialism, 142
Mathematics, 8, 11, 51
Medawar, Peter B., 58–59, 65, 66–67
Media technology, 32, 34, 136–37
Medieval Scholasticism, 7, 65, 67, 110, 120, 121
Mencken, H. L., 133
Mill, John Stuart, 162, 163
Milton, John, 25–26, 56, 121
Mind. *See* Intellect
Modernism, 11, 63, 123, 145
Mother Goose, 74–75
Music, 5

Nature, 45, 128, 132, 143, 150
Nazi ideology, 133
Nestor, King, 1–2, 6
Neuhaus, Richard John, 58
New knowledge, 70–73
New Zealand, 5
Newness, 70–73, 101, 105–10
Newspapers, 140
Newton, Sir Isaac, 7, 13, 51, 62, 79
Nietzsche, Friedrich Wilhelm, 133
Nominalism, 9, 13–14, 62

O! Calcutta, 132, 142
Occam, William of, 14, 162

O'Connor, Flannery, 58, 59
Odysseus, 66, 151
Oedipus, 35
Old age, 1–2, 81–82, 110–11
Origen, 46
Original Sin, 12, 68, 90, 108
Originality, 105–10. *See also* Newness
Ornstein, Robert, 65
Orwell, George, 47, 102

PACs. *See* Political action committees
Parain, Brice, 6, 13
Parents, 134–35. *See also* Families
Particle physics, 7–8, 10–12, 50, 62
Patriotism, 147
Paul, St., 3, 68, 83, 105, 126–27, 147
Péguy, Charles, 69
Peloponnesian states, 162
Person/personhood, 127, 138–41, 146, 156, 159, 164. *See also* Individual, individuality
Personality, 102, 159, 164
Pert stage, 112–13
Philokalos, 61–63, 65
Philosophical nominalism, 62
Philosophos, 61–65
Philosophy, 33, 42–43, 70, 73
Physics, 7–8, 9–12, 50, 53, 62
Pieper, Joseph, 105
Plants: reactions to music of, 5
Plato, 7, 9, 12, 19, 48, 55, 56, 61–65, 79, 91, 92, 93, 138
Pluralism, 94
Poe, Edgar Allan, 76–78
Poetic stage, 113
Poets, 55–64. *See also* names of specific poets
Polanyi, Michael, 65, 66
Political action committees, 163
Poll-Parrot stage, 111–12, 113
Polonius, 2
Pope, Alexander, 96
Pornography: 71, 136; intellectual, 71, 73
Post, Emily, 39
Pregnancy: teenage, 71
Prejudice, 75–76
Professionalism, 23, 29, 31–32, 37, 42, 45–46, 49. *See also* Specialization

Professors. *See* Faculty
Progress, 30, 72, 109–10
Pronunciation, 95–100
Provincialism, 27–29
Prudence, 37–44, 49
Psychology, 102
Publish-or-perish syndrome, 70–71
Punctuation, 23–24
Puritanism, 104

Quantum mechanics, 9
Quantum physics, 11

Radicalism, 134–35, 138, 139–40
Raleigh, Sir Walter, 96
Ransome, John Crowe, 38
Ratio, 67, 68, 120, 121, 122, 131, 139, 155, 156, 157, 163
Rationalism, rationality, 16, 53, 119, 123–24, 137
Realism. *See* Critical realism
Reconstruction, 27
Reductionism, 52, 54, 62, 119–20, 123, 152, 153, 154, 155
Regionalism, 27–28
Relativism, 9–11, 33, 91, 94
Religious fundamentalism, 10, 11, 51, 134–41
Republican convention (1984), 23–24
Restlessness, 93–95, 101, 108, 116
Rhetoric, 113
Robinson, A. E., 75
Rousseau, Jean Jacques, 19, 128, 142, 161, 162

Sayers, Dorothy, 73, 111–14, 122
Scholasticism: 9, 11; medieval, 7, 65, 67, 110, 120, 121
Science: metaphysics and, 7–12, 14, 49–50, 52; reason and, 8–9; fundamentalism and, 11–12; prestige of, 48; inadequacies of, 50–53; versus art, 54–55, 68, 131; mechanistic simplifications of, 62; reductionism of, 152
Secular fundamentalism, 154
Secular gnosticism, 125, 138–39, 155
Secular humanism, 137, 140–41
Secular liberalism, 136
Self-interest, 159, 160, 161, 163
Self-love, 148–51, 153, 158–60

Self-sacrifice, 159–60
Sensuality, 132
Service, 20–21
Sex education, 134–36, 144
Sexuality, 132
Shadows: versus substance, 108–10
Shakespeare, William, 19, 20, 40–42, 55, 58, 89, 96, 110
Shelley, Percy Bysshe, 47, 48, 49, 55, 56
Silence, 13, 17–18, 22, 29, 39
Single-parent family, 134
Situational ethics, 73, 91
Situational grammar, 91
Slavery, 27
Snow, C. P., 68
Social contract theory, 129, 130, 132, 141–42, 159, 161, 162–63
Socrates, 8, 46, 59, 92, 93, 125, 155, 156
Solipsism, 10, 33, 123
Song of Roland, 44
Soul, 110, 122, 151, 154, 155–57
Spacek, Sissy, 34–35
Specialization, 16, 32–35, 47–48, 49, 53–54, 92, 94
Spectacle: versus action, 32, 34–35, 43–45, 101, 133, 157–58
Spiritual nature. *See* Soul
Spock, Benjamin, 34–35
Stalin, Joseph, 160
Statue of Liberty, 26–27
Students: responsibilities of, 4, 80, 91; relationship with faculty, 6, 38–39; faculty use of first names of, 38–39; grades and, 78–79, 80; and barriers to liberal arts education, 114–18; higher education's responsibility toward, 115
Subject: and object, 123
Success, 103–104. *See also* Progress
Suicide, 153, 154–55
Surrogate parentage, 152
Swift, Jonathan, 15, 16, 28, 47
Synge, John Millington, 97

Tate, Allen, 27–28
Teachers. *See* Education; Faculty; Higher education; Liberal arts education
Technology, 45, 66

Television, 32, 136, 140
Tennyson, Alfred Lord, 56
Teresa, Mother, 160
Terrorism, 161
Thomas, Dylan, 60
Thomas, St. *See* Aquinas, St. Thomas
Thomsen, D. E., 9–10
Thucydides, 162
Tristan and Iseult, 59–60, 63, 64
Trivia, 16–17
Trivial Pursuit, 16
Trojan War, 1–2
Truth, 2, 19–20, 37, 43–44, 47, 60, 63, 64, 65, 72–73, 80, 90, 91, 105, 108. *See also* False witness; Wisdom
Tyranny, 162

Universities. *See* Higher education; Liberal arts education

Virgil, 20, 121–22
Virtue, 11, 37–44, 49, 80, 88–92, 95, 103, 105, 114
Voegelin, Eric, 50, 51, 52, 62, 65, 72

Weaver, Richard, 79
Webster, Noah, 7
Whim, 152–54

Wisdom, 1, 17–18, 61–62, 81–82. *See also* Knowledge; Truth
Woodstock, 132
Words: importance of, 2–3, 4, 13, 99–100; *bound/bind,* 3–5, 21, 28; dictionary and, 4, 6–7; subversive quality of, 6, 7; complexity of, 12–14; relation to reality, 14–16, 18; *service,* 20–21; false witness and, 46; and community of scholars, 47–48; mystery of, 75, 79; imagery and, 76–77; meanings of, 76; and education, 78–79; pronunciation of, 95–100; strange usages of, 97–98. *See also* Language
Wordsworth, William, 36, 48, 49, 56, 65, 67

Yeats, William Butler, 89, 96
Youth: compared with age, 1–2, 110–11; children in adult roles, 57–58; potential of, 102; destruction of reality and, 103; reaction to reality, 107–108; psychological development of, 111–13; suicide of, 153, 154–155
Youth movement, 131–37, 139–40, 142–43